TABLE OF CONTENTS

This book is dedicated to my wife, family, friends, business partners, customers, and employees. I wouldn't be here without you.

” Success is a journey, not a destination. The doing is often more important than the outcome.”- Arthur Ashe

2

7

INTRODUCTION

There are two types of people in this world. There are doers, and there are complainers. Which are you?

If you can get one piece of advice from this book that will help you and your business, then this book is worth every cent.

First off, I want to say thank you for purchasing this book. I tried to include everything I have learned over the last 10 years.

I have started several businesses over the years. Some have failed and some have succeeded. The funny thing is the business I stuck with no matter what was the business that succeeded. The ups the downs, the days I wanted to quit, because I was, and still am, overwhelmed. In business you need to have thick skin and be able to take a beating. But you also need the heart to get back up.

The business I wanted to give up on countless times but didn't, now does high 6 to low 7 figures per year. And with each year we continue to grow. Success in my business happened around the 18-to-24-month mark. If I had quit around 16 months, I would have never known how successful we would be, and I would have missed out on our true potential.

Like Mark Cuban says, "You only need to get it right once." If you haven't read or listened to his book "*How to Win at the Game of Life*." You're missing out. How often do you get to listen to a billionaire talk about where he grew up, what he did in his 20s and 30s, and how he became the humble family man he is today? Mark also talks about how he started and grew a couple of his businesses. The ups and downs of what an entrepreneur goes through daily. And he reads the audio book himself. The book is like a reminder that anyone can do it.

About me

Do I know it all? No. But what I have learned I am going to share with you. One thing I hate about books is trying to find good stuff. I have bought over a hundred books, and then I start reading the book, about 5 minutes in, I am like what is this garbage. Just a bunch of nonsense and needless information. Now, I do find some good ones. But it feels like 1 out of 5 is mostly nonsense. A bunch of words that don't really mean anything and never give direction or action steps. In this book I try to paint a picture of what I have learned over the last 10 years. Being a successful business owner is not a destination, it is a journey. A constant evolution of self-development and personal growth. With each day you add a new layer. Learn a new strategy or build a little more confidence.

I hate to break it to you, there is no magic bullet get rich quick scheme. Success takes time. The best way to describe it is, creating a subconscious routine and belief system, to where you don't think about what you are doing, you just do it. That's where this book comes in. At each stage of your entrepreneurial journey, you will be hit with different problems.

Each chapter is meant to cover the different areas you might struggle in. I try to keep chapters simple and to the point. But if you need more elaboration don't be afraid to reach out to me. I am here to help.

Also, I hear or read, people complain about the author trying to upsell you. Well, if you complain, then you don't understand basic sales. That is the first thing they teach you in sales school. "Do you want fries with that", ring a bell. I personally know it is rehashing.

You make a sale and then ask if they want to buy another item. Depending on how many items you have you can do a lot of upselling. Finding items that complement each other can 2x, 3x or even 4x your business.

Now if the author gives you nothing of value, and still asks for you to visit his or her site, then that's different. An author should provide real value in their book before they upsell you.

I know reading this book you will get a ton of value and it will be worth every cent you spend. My upsell will be my book list. On the book list you will find books that I have personally read. The only one that I used in the updated version was in the book for dummies. Other than that, the books listed have helped me in some way and I think they are worth sharing.

https://www.omnisquared.com/books-for-growing-your-business

I do have it linked to Amazon affiliates but that is not the reason I am telling you about it. I am telling you because I only add books, I think are worthy of making it to the list. Now, would I be a salesperson if I didn't try to upsell? Probably not. But it is free publicity for a page that doesn't get many views because nobody knows me. Why not try and make a few bucks for helping others?

The good thing about this book is I don't need to upsell anything. This book should be packed full of ideas and steps that can help you right now. Now I might have some recommendations, but I am not affiliated with any of the products or software I mention.

I might start a resources tab, or Facebook page to help put out more content. That is only because if the book is published, I cannot go back and keep adding stuff.

I want this book to be one of the best beginners to advanced business books you can get. I tried to break down everything I learned into small easy-to-follow chapters. But let's face it, I am not perfect. Not everyone will enjoy the book, although, I hope everyone does.

If you do like the book leave a review. It will help the book get seen and in return will help others. If you want to talk, email me at omnisquared88@gmail.com, or just Google me, and I will come right up.

Why am I doing this? I wanted to write a book that helped people. And teach in a way that someone could absorb and implement the tips and strategies into their lives today. A book that could provide immediate help and guidance.

If you have ever wondered what sets a successful business apart from a failing business, you're not alone. A successful business owner master's the topics mentioned in this book.

Now, only some things will apply to everyone or every business. Not every business will be talked about. But the fundamental steps remain the same. Becoming a successful entrepreneur means building a solid foundation for yourself no matter what business you're in. This book is to help you build the characteristics and foundation of a successful business owner. You can come back to the book every so often for a refresher on what to do.

Rome wasn't built in a day. It takes time. Build layer upon layer. Like Will Smith said. "Brick by brick, building a wall no one can break."

My back story

I wasn't born into a good home. I didn't have direction in my life until I was 30. I could care less where I was going to sleep, what I was going to eat and what I was going to do. That all changed after I turned 30 and moved out on my own. Up until that time I had roommates to turn to, or couches to crash on.

After my pivot in life, I gravitated towards some of the most fascinating people in the modern time. I have learned from some of the greatest minds in the world. Studied them even, but nothing is like *failing, reflecting, and moving forward.*

I also wanted to add this somewhere in the book. This is a shot out to someone I have never met but have spent days watching and listening to, Ed Mylet. He said this in a video one time, and I am paraphrasing. He said, "Forget multiple streams of income. Get good at one thing. If I start a business, I am going to have laser focus and funnel all my attention and energy into one business. Not 3 or 4 businesses. And I am going to kick your ass in that industry."

That is the intensity you need if you are going to succeed. Whatever you do, go for it 100%. Don't half-ass it.

And if you're saying, why would I half-ass it? It's because we have bad days. Or you have an exit strategy if things don't work out. A deal didn't go through, rude customers. In business a lot will get you down. Building a successful business takes discipline. Discipline to get up every day and give it your all. Remember, grab a bull by the horns, and GO FOR IT! BURN THE BOATS!

Where I started

In 2013 or so I started a course that changed my life. It was a random YouTube ad. The course was the 67 steps by Tai Lopez. Some people might not like Tai for whatever reason, but he helped me. I was a believer. I started building confidence and direction from all the videos I watched.

What I liked most about the course is he took all these bits and pieces of other people's teachings and put them together into easy-to-follow videos.

Now, would I be where I am today if I didn't spend the $67 bucks? Probably not. But the point is, don't be afraid to try something because you're worried about being judged. Believing in yourself will give you the advantage you need to win.

That one road you take can take you on a path to the top. Find the motivation to try new things and develop your entrepreneurial spirit. Not everything will pan out. But you will never know unless you try? It's like a building playbook. Increasing and adjusting your plays until they are executed perfectly.

As the famous saying goes, *"The journey of a thousand miles starts with the first step."* by Lao Tzu. Without taking that first step, the journey will never begin.

And for less than a weeks' worth of coffee at Starbucks you can learn and develop a foundation to grow and achieve anything you want. Or at least open your mind to the possibilities and strategies that have helped me.

After I watched 67 steps, I started a social media site. And let me tell you it was a disaster. It was 2013 and I had no design/coding skills. The layout, the message feature, all garbage. It also had a horrible name that I changed multiple times. Then I decided to stop. Because I didn't have much success.

In between the failed social media site and my current 7 figure business, I tried everything, blogs, e-commerce, YouTube, and courses. And I never found anything that worked. Except for one Google Ads course. It was done well. But it would be outdated 3 months later because Google Ads is constantly changing. And I did sell a few products at my e-com store, but Covid hit, and I couldn't get anything imported, so I gave up.
Looking back, I should have bought in bulk. But lesson learned! Then I wrote a quick book on budgeting and saving. That does well, and I still get sales from it today.

Now, fast forward to around 2019 and I am running a multimillion-dollar low-voltage division for a well-known company in my area. I got to learn the business side of construction from the owner and my boss. I was basically 3rd in command for our division.

The main thing I learned from the President was how to create, build, and grow relationships. Well at least that's what I knew you had to do. But actually, doing that is the hard part.

My manager knew how to do the work and did it well. Between the 2, I could learn a lot about business. I was in that position for about 2.5 years.

After years of asking my manager to start our own business, he finally said yes. Not because I convinced him, but because we weren't treated fairly. The office had a vibe about it, and it wasn't fun to come to work. Some other things happened and are not my place to talk about.

As of August 2020, our company was officially born. Now it's time to take everything I have learned and share it with you. In my own direct approach kind of way.

This book is everything that I have learned in the last 10 years. Which can help you for many more years to come. I have run multi-million-dollar divisions. I have built 6 and 7-figure companies. And I am going to teach you everything I know.

This book is not like other books that purely talk about examples of other books or studies people read. Or where the author goes round and round but never actually says anything. Or the author purely talks about other people's experiences that they read about.

I do have a few references, but this book is mainly about my business, and what I have learned and figured out. This is unlike any other book I have seen. And it is my own opinion, perspective, and experience, so it might not be for everyone.

I will let you know that I am in a service-based industry, so many of my examples will be used to help that style of business.

Please enjoy. And reach out to me with any questions or comments. If you run into any spelling or grammar errors, I apologize in advance.

My views and opinions

This book is not like any other book, it is about my life and what I learned. Not someone else. Not some study done, not an interpretation of someone else's journey. This book is based on my thoughts, weaknesses, and strengths.

And what is the best experience for learning? Doing it for yourself. The only issue is translating my thoughts onto paper for you to read and understand. I have had a couple head injuries when I was growing up. And I am also left-handed. That could be why I think differently than most people. I add a different perspective.

But I tried to break the norm and give actual steps anyone can take to succeed. I also have a ton of empathy. So much, I cannot listen to a story about surgery or a knife accident without feeling like it happens to me. I think this came from not talking as much and playing off people's body language and energy when I was younger.

I don't have degrees; I have a successful business. That I built from the ground up and very little money. I grew up poor. If I asked for $5 I was turned down. Not because they didn't have it, but because they thought I didn't deserve it.

If you asked me 20 years ago if I would own a home, have money in the bank, 2 paid off cars, a payroll so big it would make any beginner entrepreneur squirm. I would have laughed at you.

With that being said, I hope you enjoy this book and get some value from it.

Message me with any questions you have omnisquared88@gmail.com

16

Chapter 1: Building Confidence

I want to start this book by talking about confidence. Confidence is a basic skill that can be taught. If confidence can be taught, then it can also be learned. It is often a skill that needs to be developed over time. I cannot express the importance of confidence enough, and that is why it is the first chapter in this book.

Confidence is a core skill in your foundation of being an entrepreneur. Confidence will open doors for you like you never thought possible.

In the book *Outliers by Malcolm Gladwell*, he talks about people that stand out from the masses. The 1% in achievement. And one thing was proven. Wealthy people tend to empower their kids with confidence and positivity.

Wealthy families encourage their kids to try new things from a young age. If a wealthy child wants to start dancing, soccer and swimming, the wealthy parents will encourage the child to try all 3.

Wealthy kids are not held back by limitations such as money, or negative attitudes.

So, on the one hand, you have a wealthy encouraging family, and on the other hand, you have a poor, negative thought family. Now, not all poor families are negative in the sense of values.

More in the sense of encouragement and financial resources. And this is not a 100% rule. Some poor families can see potential in the child and scrape every cent for that child to have a shot at being happy.

But in the book, research showed poor parents do not encourage the child to try new things. Therefore, the child lacks the courage and confidence to try new things, and is essentially afraid of failure. Since this was the way my home operated, this part of the book hit home for me. I have wanted to try hockey for years. But my mom could not afford it.

She was a single mom who worked the graveyard shift as a security guard and then moved into a position as a loan officer at a local bank. When I asked for something like playing hockey, I was met with a firm no. Chances are it was probably an expensive sport. You need pads, skates, sticks and so on.

Also, my mom probably knew nothing about hockey. We were a football baseball family. My mom could have been acting on her subconscious auto pilot and rejected anything new, because that is what she was taught. But whatever the reason, it was a no.

When a child is told no their entire life, they will have a huge hill to climb if they want to change their life from a no mindset to a yes mindset.

The rich kid tries new sports, and the poor kid is told they can't afford it. When we are at our early stages of life, these traits can become routine and engrained in our subconscious.

In order to change a deep-rooted program, you must convince yourself. The few ways that I have found to convince myself is to use repetition and affirmations. Day in and day out, constantly training myself, and saying things like, "I can, I am, I will'. For every no, we must tell ourselves yes 100 times before it makes a dent.

You must tell yourself so many times that you believe it. We are attempting to rewrite our original coding that is mixed in with our heartbeat and breathing. These programs are tucked away in our subconscious and for good reason. We need programming to survive. But that doesn't mean we can't rewrite a part of the code to work in our favor.

Confidence vs arrogance

Now, confidence can be learned. But you must be able to tell the difference in how you come across to other people.

Confidence is going to be the most used item in your tool bag, but it can be confused with arrogance. Confidence is not arrogance. Arrogance is not confidence.

In my opinion, arrogance is an energy you project. Arrogance can be taken in many ways. I was guilty of being arrogant for years and wondered why some people were put off by my attitude. They thought, I thought, I was better than them or something like that. But that couldn't be farther from the truth.

I was excited to be alive and enjoying life. You can't get any more real than that. But some people didn't like it. It would come off as strange or cocky. Nobody likes cocky. Especially the bosses and owners.

And yes, I had no fear. I was arrogant. I grew up in a small city and when I was 16 we had boxing matches after work or at lunch. I was also in the Marines for a short while before I got discharged for lying on my application. On top of all that, I was young and in my twenties with nothing to lose.

People don't like being arrogant, I suggest you look inside and see what you project. It might not be arrogance, it could be self-doubt, or even an anxious feeling. A good practice for entrepreneurs is to look inside themselves. Figure out the strengths and weaknesses.

Be honest with yourself. And if needed, get feedback from others.

Projecting confidence

Now when you project confidence, people take it differently. You think quickly, and project trust. This one little tweak, perfected, can be a game changer in business. But it must come naturally and not forced. You won't get it right every time or with everyone. But you will start to see people's attitude change. And it will be easier to talk to customers.

On top of confidence, you will need to build rapport with customers and clients. Rapport is a strategy people use in sales and customer service. Building rapport is like starting a friendship and finding similar interests between the two parties. The best analogy I can think of is a sports team. When you're at a sports game and two people meet for the first time, it is easier and more comfortable knowing you both like the same team. Conversation can flow more freely.

Building rapport is about having similar interests as the other person. People want to do business with people they like. Building rapport is a byproduct of confidence. It is easier to build when you believe in yourself, hobbies and likes.

Like I said earlier, do not force it. Let it come natural, timing is everything. Let the conversation flow.

Affirmations

Not all of us will come from a rich family. And if you do come from a rich family, this chapter might enable you to see life from a different perspective.

If you come from a poor family, chances are, you will need to change programming on a subconscious level.

I must remind myself every day that I am smart, funny, and reliable. I say my affirmations, morning noon, and night and every other time in between. You will need to convince yourself that you have what it takes on all levels to succeed. For most, this will take time. Most likely years. So, I would start as soon as possible.

Because I was called things like, shut up and stupid at a very early age. I was afraid to talk most of my early childhood. On one hand I have confidence in my physical ability, on the other hand my mental ability is as beat down as they come.

How to build confidence other than affirmations?

Confidence is an "I know my position inside and out and I won't let you down", attitude.

Learn everything you can about your business. This can help you build confidence in your ability to provide the best service for your customer or client. A restaurant owner should know their menu inside and out. What drinks are on tap, the hours, the staff names, the customer names. And so on. Learn it all, and you will be admired by others.

Any service-based business will need to know the answers to most questions without hesitation. That's what builds trust. That is when your customer will relax and drop their guard.

Confidence is the single most used tool in an entrepreneur's tool bag. confidence is used every day, all day. On the phone, in person or by email.

The Wolf of Wall Street: Jordan Belfort said it best, *"You must transfer your confidence like a furnace transfers heat. You cannot heat the house if the furnace is broken."*

This is something that has stuck with me. Building confidence will take time. You will need to build on what confidence you do have until you can walk into a meeting, hold your head high and sell yourself and your business.

Or you might need to fake it until you make it. But that's okay. Like Dan Pena says, *"go sit in the Rolls Royce, and you will start to think you deserve that car"*. I am paraphrasing, but the principle has the same meaning.

What Dan is saying is by doing something that is tangible, something you can physically hold in your hands. You can change your life. Because you believe you can do it. You start to believe you are worth it.

I did this. I went to an exotic car dealership. I asked to sit in a $170,000 Lambo. I imagined I was in my driveway getting into my car and it was mine. It felt good. I could visualize myself. From the research I have read, the mind doesn't know what's real and what's not. The mind sees you getting in and out of an expensive car.

In my opinion, the mind sees a vision. And keeping that vision is like writing down your affirmation.

Now sitting in an exotic car is another way to build confidence. I didn't think about this at the time and how the two were connected. I was hesitant and uncertain if I should ask. I had to build the courage up just to sit in the car. I had to tell myself, I deserve this, I can afford it, I need to ask. Mainly I needed to ask because all the cars were locked. Or I would have just sat in them. But asking to sit in a $170,000 Lambo takes self-esteem. It takes confidence. I'm interested if anyone reading this will try it. And what emotions and feelings did you encounter? Let me know!

Celebrate the small wins

Confidence has a lot of different levels. Another way to start building confidence is to celebrate the small wins. Give yourself a pat on the back when you complete the smallest accomplishments.

A lot of self-confidence comes with repetition. Rewiring your brain to believe you are worth it and you can succeed. Congratulate yourself no matter how small the accomplishment is. One aspect of confidence in my opinion is love. More specifically, loving yourself. If you don't love yourself, it might be difficult to build the confidence you need to succeed.

Try new things and complete them. Follow through until the end.

Our minds as business owners are a little different than the average 9-5 worker. We have a sense of blind hope that carries us to start and try new things. Take that ball of hope and what self-confidence you have in one aspect of your life and transfer it to other areas of your life.

What are some areas of your life that you are confident in? Is it in being a father, or maybe a sport you play. Or it could be a subject or even a video game. Take whatever confidence you have and transfer it to another area of your life.

When I say transfer confidence what I mean is don't be afraid to try new things. If you can be good at one thing, with a little practice and effort you can be good at other things. Chances are you don't pick up a bat and ball and become an all-star. You must put in the time and effort.

You won't know your true potential until you try. In the next chapter I am going to teach you how to build confidence in areas of your life you never thought possible.

One way to build confidence is through failure and repetition, and by mastering the basics! That leads us into our next chapter.

What are some areas that you lack confidence in?

What are some areas that you have confidence in?

What can you do to build confidence in the areas you are lacking?

24

Chapter 2: The Basics

I wanted to put this chapter early in the book. Because I feel mastering the basics can truly help you in business. And should be another core component in your foundation.

I did not come up with this process, I owe the credit to Alan Stein Jr, and his book "*Raise Your Game*". I highly recommend you check it out.

Now, Alan talks about a morning when he meets Kobe Bryant for practice. Alan was all pumped and wanted to get to the practice early to show he meant business. Alan arrived about 3:30 am. Alan was amazed when he showed up to the gym.

Kobe was already in the gym practicing and was in a full sweat. Kobe was in his warmup session and getting ready for the practice session. He said he watched one of the best players in the world do the most basic drills.

Okay, so how does this apply to you? Well, if you want to be a master of your craft, then you need to master the basics as well. It does not matter who and what you do. If you want to be the best, you must master the basics.

Kobe was arguably one of the best basketball players of all time. But that didn't stop him from practicing even the most basic drills.

So how do you master the basics of your craft? Let's boil this down to a few simple topics. And this will work for any business. Get a pen and paper or a notepad on a laptop or computer. And start writing down what the basics are for your business.

The basics

Let's say I am in construction, and I am the owner. What would my basics be? That depends on the jobs you are doing. Since I do everything at my company my basics are:

Sales
Estimating (learning about the material, labor and floor layouts)
Employee rapport
Laws
Taxes
Marketing and advertising
Hiring
HR

I could probably go on and on, but I think you get the point. Now, let's start with sales. Making sales is the lifeblood of our business. Why? Because if you don't have sales, you're not going to have money coming in. If you don't have money coming in, you probably won't have money to pay your bills. You will be working long days and nights trying to make your savings stretch.

Gary Keller talks about "The One Thing". This was a book a read years ago. It stuck with me. What he said is you need to focus on one thing. My one thing and has always been my one thing is sales. I base my entire company around sales.

If I don't make sales, my employees can't work. If I don't make sales, I don't eat. If I don't make sales, I can't take vacations. And so on. Without sales, what is the point of being in business?

Let's break sales down to some of the basics.

Customer rapport
Knowledge and expertise of your products
Confidence, not arrogance
Vocabulary
Nurturing and follow up
Punctuality
Grammer

These are some simple topics that you can work on every day to become an expert in sales. It takes 5 minutes to break down a job title you think you will need to develop to be successful. When you master the basics of a specific job title you will end up being a master of that craft. Which in return is priceless. And will pay you for years to come.

Let's do another one. Marketing! One of my favorite things to do.

The basics of marketing and advertising:

Copy your successful competitors
Web design
Contact forms
Branded email
Business cards
Hooks to catch people's attention
Colors

SEO
Landing pages
What sites to advertise on (we will cover this in a later chapter as well)

Web design

WordPress and Elementor or are a great combination. You can go to your competitor's sites for inspiration. Watch a couple of how-to videos on Elementor and you're off. You can do templates, and with the latest updates it is even easier to make nice easy to use websites.

Another reason I like WordPress is you have more control over what your site does. For instance, you download a plugin called Yoast SEO and it literally helps you out with SEO. Even the free version. I have pages ranked on the first page of Google using the free plugin. If you're not sure what a plugin is, it is basically a file you download/upload to your site. It works in the way an app would work on a phone. It allows you some form of function or tool that you can use on your site.

Some plugins might not be compatible with your version or theme, but WordPress will let you know before you download/upload.

Plugins

Some plugins are easy to use and activate. They are just as easy to remove. I'll stick with Yoast SEO for example. If you go to create a page, and if Yoast is active, you can scroll to the bottom of the page and see items in red. That is Yoast telling you exactly what to do so your page is more user-friendly for a Google search. This is a easy to do step and will set you up for the long game.

You might have to Google a few terms here and there, but it is a basic tool anyone can use. But not everyone does. This one basic thing can help you generate $50,000.00 in one contract (I know from experience) or get brought up in searches for whatever your business is and land deals, customers, or contracts to build your pipeline. It is the basics of SEO!

Website colors

The colors are as basic as you can get. But will you take the time to see what colors go with other colors? For instance, gray and blue are our colors. Go to a color chart and pick your colors. Look up color pallets and see what colors work together. And if you want, look up what emotions colors make.

Colors could be a bid part of your company and brand. If you're in it for the long hall, you will want to pick your colors wisely.

Hooks

Hooks are a basic marketing/advertising term. It means to catch someone's attention with a few words. Do a Google search and see what your competitors are saying in ads. Look them up on Facebook, Instagram, etc. I try to stay with local competition. I feel it is already working in my area so why change it. If I am in San Francisco, I won't try to copy people in Texas. I am not saying that either one is better, but why not go with what is working in your area?

For instance, look up #1 Rated Lawyer in your town and state. See what they are putting in headlines and meta description. This is a basic technique that you can use for brainstorming topics, pages or ads for your company. Now, do not copy word for word. Switch it up. Look for little things like #1, or Top Rated, key words that grab attention.

You want to hook customers and clients within a few seconds, something that catches their eye.

Business cards

Business cards are another basic advertising and marketing tool that not everyone does. But it works. Meeting new customers, and referrals, all can come with a simple business card. A good quality card does stand out. Look up designs for inspiration. I landed 2 very large deals with just one business card.

I gave my card out on a job site, a few months later I got invited to bid on a few projects. We went tight and won 2 of the 3 projects. The total for the two projects was some of the biggest projects we have ever landed. And it all started with handing out my business card.

I paid $60 bucks for a software program called *Affinity Designer*. Not sure if the deal is still around but I have it for life and never have to buy it again. I resize photos to work on my site and make business cards, flyers, and t-shirt designs. All-in-one software.

By now, I am sure you get the point. Break down every category in your business, into simple easy-to-do things and learn to master them. You will increase sales, conversions, and confidence. Things take time, and it is easier to digest smaller bites.

Outsourcing

Now, I get it, some of these items and tasks can be outsourced. But if you don't have the money, then chances are you have the time to learn them. I will touch on this topic later, but I will briefly mention it here as well.

If you have enough capital to hire someone that is a master of their craft, then that is a workaround you can do. But not everyone has the capital to do that. Hiring the best takes a lot of financial resources, but it is the most strategic way to build a company.

Now if you haven't broken down your workflow into categories and then broken those categories down into basic skill sets, then go ahead and do that now! You will be glad you did!

What can you outsource? I outsourced our HR for $300 a month. Once you start getting more and more employees, you will want to make sure you're covered. I was told by the company that we outsource from, that they know a company that gets sued a lot. And they thought it was normal.

After you break down your category and skill needed, figure out what the basics are to build that skill. Then practice that skill until you get it right.

Mastering the basics is going to allow your company to go from good to elite.

What I lacked

One skill that I lacked was project management. Now you might think how I can run a successful company and lack project management. When I worked at my old company, I was an estimator. I oversaw ordering, estimating, customer service, meetings and made sure the project was completed the way it was designed.

But the things I did not do were work with the crew, get basic material for them, schedule them, or answer questions. We had a superintendent that would help out and take care of the daily things. I was overseeing the Superintendent. My contact with the crew was minimal.

Now when you're at a big company you get a ton of support, We have a dedicated HR person, dedicated parts person, dedicated accountant. Those are huge blessings that you don't think of when you start your own company.

Everything you need to have and grow a successful business. Now at my company, we had me. Filling in those gaps is and was difficult. But what I have learned is to listen and reflect.

Now I have material prepared for my team. I make sure they have everything they need before they start a project. I might miss a few things like screws, but the bulk of material is ready to go.

I make sure I have them scheduled and I go out of my way to make sure they take care of even the smallest things. You would not believe how many parts it takes to complete even the most basic job.

I am becoming a master project manager. Now by me doing that, my crew can be more efficient, and I can lead by example, and in return our projects are more successful.

I am curious how you broke down your position to its most basic form. What did you come up with?

33

Chapter 3: Building Relationships

This is one of the most important aspects of ANY business. Building relationships with people that surround you. Customers, clients, employees, family, and friends.

Well, you might be asking, okay, how do I build relationships? That is a question for the ages. And a tough one to master. But it can be done. Relationships, at their most basic level, are connections and trust.

Connecting with people is an art that any entrepreneur, businessperson, or salesperson will need to master to become successful. Or you will need to hire someone to do it for you. There is a reason why salespeople are one of the highest paid. Sales generate income, which creates profit.

I have been working on this trait for a few years now and have been getting better and better with each interaction I have. I was just on a call with another business owner. I was reaching out because we needed a product they sell. And at the start of the conversation, he mentioned that he had an injury. I asked a simple question about what happened and after 10 minutes he was wondering how we got on the topic of him snowboarding for 15 years.

Good relationship building is breaking down the walls and allowing a friendship to form.

Now, there is a caveat to this skill that you are building. You must be genuinely interested in the people that you're talking to. Most people can tell if you're not being genuine.

Like anything else in life, it will take time. One way to practice this skill set is to build relationships with strangers you meet in public and who have nothing to do with your business. That way you develop a genuine interest in other people, rather than trying to sell them. Nobody likes to get sold. When people are pushy, I shut down and lose interest fast.

My guard goes up and I try anything I can to get off the phone or out the door.

Barbers are a great way to test out conversation starters and build connections with people. Ask a question and listen.

Listening is an under rated skill that allows people to talk. And what do people like most in a conversation? To talk about themselves.

This skill will come in handy when you meet a customer for the first time either in person or over the phone.

You will build *confidence* in yourself when meeting and talking with strangers. Which will have a snowball effect. Overtime this skill will come naturally. The more reps you put in the easier it gets. Look for any interaction with a person you don't know in your day-to-day life and try to build a connection with them.

Listen to others

Okay, now let's talk more about listening to the person you're interacting with. We all know we should do it, but do we? I know people that like to hear themselves talk and when I talk, they don't listen. They are waiting for their turn to talk again. This can be annoying and frustrating.

When you ask a question, listen with intent. For instance, I asked a question to the salesperson I was on a Zoom call with. I said, what are you doing for marketing and advertising, how are you driving leads for your business?

If someone has experience in a skill that you are trying to build, ask the question you need help with. If that person is also passionate about that skill, you will learn a lot in just a few minutes.

When I asked the marketing and advertising question, I was genuinely interested in what they had to say. I was eager to hear every word and take notes. About 15 minutes later, he said, "Wow, I am rambling on". In other words, he was in the zone and was sharing knowledge that is hard to find or read in a book.

Now would I use every tip I heard? Probably not, but that conversation can help me brainstorm other marketing and advertising ideas that I can relate to my business. That would drive traffic to my business and in return would increase profits. I mean we are all in this to make some money right?

If we break down relationship building to its most simple characteristics, listening is on the list. Master listing and you will be one step closer to mastering relationships.

Master of your craft

Another way to build relationships and I see this time and time again. Is to be an expert in the field your business is in, and people will come to you for advice. It's really that simple.

Mark Cuban says that he is one of the most prepared people in a meeting. And it's simple to pick up an owner's manual of the product you are selling and learn all about it. He also says that most people will not pick up the manual and that is what gives you the advantage.

Knowledge is power.

Here is another example of knowing your products and how it can help you build and strengthen relationships.

I had a job walk with a customer and we were talking about power for a card access system. I mentioned that he would need an external power supply. I didn't think much of it at the time. I was pointing out something that I would normally think of when I would design a job.

I got a call a few weeks later, we won the job! When I went to do the job, he told me why we won. He said we won because nobody else mentioned he needed to purchase a power supply to complete the job. By being a expert in my field and having that knowledge come naturally, I was able to land another contract and build my customers' confidence in a new relationship.

That person just so happens to be the head IT person for a multibillion-dollar company. And we have done many successful projects since then. He can trust I know my stuff and know he can count on me to make each job we do successful.

On top of completing a project and looking good to the customer. Your customer will look good to their company and build trust that they can complete difficult projects.

These tips are not hard to do, but they will take time to build. Never hold back. Give it your all and always make sure you are giving 100% to your customers.

Never talk bad about anyone including a competitor

None of your customers are going to want to hear you talk badly about anyone. Always keep a positive attitude and you will strengthen relationships. I have a competitor that I want to beat every time we bid against them. But I never talk badly to a customer about them.

I always say something like, they are great company, and I understand why you made the choice you made. Even if I lose a million-dollar job to them, I play nice. And yes, I have come close to losing a million-dollar job to a competitor.

I did mention that they were missing several items in the estimate. I knew they were missing items because I was a couple hundred thousand dollars higher on a bid. That only happens if someone misses something. I knew I had everything covered. And it was true, but I never put anyone down.

And don't put other people or companies down. This is a huge tip. I know some people that do put others down. And what does that say about that person?

To me it screams insecure. And when people are insecure, they make mistakes. Customers don't want you to trash talk to others. It is negative, and childish.

Relationships take time, some longer than others.

Relationships can take time. It's simple in theory, but it takes time to build trust and rapport. Not everything is immediate, and building quality relationships takes time.

If you have tried to work with a customer or client and haven't got anywhere, be patient. Hold out as long as you can. Stay positive and stay patient. Give it a little bit longer. A few more days and a few more tries. As Ed Mylett says, "Just one more day".

I have a little story to tell that might help you. When I started my company, I reached out to a large general contractor. I was invited to quote a few projects. Some were small, and some were large. Probably 3 or 4 projects in the first year, and maybe 3 or 4 in the second year.

The only thing that I received for the weeks of work that I put in was a thank you for the estimate, we are not using you. Did I get discouraged? Yes. But did I give up? **No.** I kept trying.

Then in year 3 I finally reached out to the contractor and asked what I could do better. He said that my price was a little high on a couple projects. And on another project my number was good, but we didn't win because the project lost funding.

Feedback is so powerful and allows us to gage where we are and how we can be better. If you're not constantly getting better your company might get stagnant. And you can miss out on sales.

What I learned from that one conversation helped us grow to be big players in our city and taught me what I needed to do to land more contracts. I need to always be competitive and most importantly, never give up.

If I had given up like most people, I would have never learned how to improve myself, and I would have never landed the 4 large contracts with that company. Now my partner wanted to move on, he didn't see the point in trying. And I am glad I didn't listen.

I stuck with it. Stayed positive. And stayed in front of my customers, the timing was right. And now we are working with a large contractor in our area. I also have another quick story. About another large contactor. If you're not familiar with general contractors, they oversee construction projects.

Often times they get a project and hire a sub-contractor, which is us. And when you build a relationship with a GC you have a better chance of winning.
Okay, so I asked the contractor the same thing, why we have not won and what we can do better.

The feedback again was priceless. We were competitive in our price, but most of the projects lost funding. That lets me know that we are on the right track and have a chance to land more projects.

Be patient, know your stuff, learn from your mistakes, and be there when the time is right. You will be happy if you hang in there. And ask for feedback, people like telling you what you can do better.

Personality types and characteristics

I think understanding the person you are working with is a basic approach to relationships. You can go deep on this and really try and figure out personality types or you can do as I do and look out for a few key things. In this section I am going to cover what I look for when I work with a new customer.

For instance, are they talking slow, or fast? Are they asking questions? Are they engaged? Do they have a boss to answer or are they the decision maker?

I got a call today from a referral, it was an interesting conversation. A few weeks prior a vendor asked me if I wanted to take on a new project and they would introduce me to the customer. I said yes and started working with the customer. I let them know I needed to look at the project before I could give a price. There are too many variables when installing a security system.

The customer agreed and we set a date and time. I told the customer that it would be $125 for me to look. The person I was talking with said they would pass the cost up to management and let me know.

I received an email a few days later and the manager wanted me to drop my price. I let the customer know that I had to pay for labor and fuel, and I couldn't travel out of town for free.

I also let the customer know since they were a referral, I was already giving them a good price. But if needed I can take off $25.

Did I want to? No, but I want them to know I care and will help if I can. Would it be a loss? Not really, but it would put me closer to breaking even. I really did give them a good deal. It was a 1.5-hour round trip and a complex job I would need to walk.

Then the customer didn't want to pay for the job walk, so they sent videos. The videos were blurry, and it was hard to make out a few things. This is a very cheap customer. Cheap customers are the worst, they are looking for a deal and want to grind you down.

What I think is key to handling cheap customers is to not waste too much time. Chances are they are shopping for a number and want things as cheap as possible. And that is fine, that will happen. But being able to tell the difference and listen to the type of customer you are working with will save a lot of time and frustration.

A few years ago, I would have tried to get the project. Now I see the issues I would face and try to navigate the situation as best as possible. One thing I noticed is that when I charge a job walk fee, it eliminates me wasting my time. If the customer does not want to pay for the job walk, chances are they don't understand that you are an expert and need to be paid for your time.

Let them go with a company that doesn't charge for their time, and chances are they will get what they pay for. A poorly run company. A company that cuts corners. That's not us.

If they insist on not paying, try to give them a fair number based on the info you do have. Let them shop for the number and see if you win. Chances are any number they get will be similar in price and you still might have a shot. Don't dwell. Move on to another project.

Back to the referral, what the customer doesn't know is if they would have paid the $125 up front, and I got to see what I was doing, instead of trying to see from a blurry video. I could have gone tighter on my number and gave them a price for the entire job. But since I had to go off a video, I had to turn down part of the work.

But do I really want a job where the customer is going to grind me down? Probably not. Do I want to lose money and not make a profit because the customer is cheap? No, definitely not. And I don't want to burn a bridge either, no matter how small or large a project is.

Even cheap relationships can pay you for years to come. Understanding the person, you are working with is key. Here is a huge tip for service-based business, ALWAYS GIVE YOUR BEST NUMBER!

Conclusion

Don't be afraid to fail. And if you do fail, reflect. Reflect on everything. Then try again. One thing I did on job walks was I said the wrong thing. I say some random thing and make it super awkward. The only way I knew what I did and how to fix it was to reflect and tell myself not to do that.

It happened 4 or 5 times on different job walks and then it started to stick. It came naturally not to say the wrong thing or hold my tongue. Now, I am winning jobs and saying the right thing.

But I also had to learn that when I win a job, and complete it, not to say the wrong thing. I did this 3 times in a row. Working directly for a customer can be tricky.

You need to learn to never say the wrong thing, ever. Even after a job is done. Because you want the next job. If you mess up and say something dumb, doesn't matter how smooth the job went. Your customer won't want to call you back.

Don't get discouraged even if you start a conversation with a barista and it goes bad. That's why you are practicing. So, when you meet a customer, you get a few of the bad interactions out of the way. Now, you are not going to get along with everyone for a million reasons.

Maybe they had a bad day or didn't like something you said. Don't worry, recover, and move on. Depending on your business, relationships could either make you or break you. Most multi-million-dollar businesses know this. Repeat customers could be a large portion of your bottom line.

Let's say you own a restaurant; you must build a relationship with your customer base. The foundation is simple. Always take care of your customers. If an employee is rude to the customer, apologize.

Let them know you will talk to the employee. Give the employee a chance to correct his or her behavior. A second time and that employee might need to be let go. As for your customers, they deserve a free meal on the house, and maybe a free meal the next time they come in.

Business is competitive, don't give your customers reasons to leave and go to your competition.

Many commercial and residential companies build their businesses on relationships. A general contractor and the customer, a subcontractor and general contractor. These relationships are cultivated over years of hard work. Do not underestimate the power of the relationship.

People want to do business with people they like. Remember that. Your job is to get better and better each day. Build a solid foundation on relationships and the chances are you will succeed.

What can you do to start building relationships?

Who can you start up a conversation with and be genuinely interested in?

45

Chapter 4: Preparation

I decided to dedicate a whole chapter of this book to preparation. This could be the single most important thing you do when trying to build relationships and grow your business.

This can be true for any field. For instance, let's say you are in the insurance business. You get a lead on your site, let's call them Jim. Jim wants term life insurance. You're a new agent. What do you do?

What do you think would have the most beneficial impact on your conversation with Jim?

Going into the conversation and not knowing anything about term life insurance?

Or learn term life better than anyone?

What would you say is the best way to go about your first interaction with a new customer? Being over-prepared or being under-prepared?

Okay, here is another example. This is relatable to my field. Let's say you're in construction. You are a new business owner. You have a complex project and have been invited to a meeting with the owner or owner's rep.

The night before, go through the plans, go through the spec, go through the notes. Double-check and triple-check everything. When you enter the meeting, you know everything about the scope of the project and all the paperwork is completed correctly.

Do you think the owner or owner's rep will appreciate you being prepared for your meeting? Of course, they would. Chances are your competition will lack in this area and you will be able to shine.

I am not familiar with other scopes on a construction project, so I am unaware of how complex they are. I am in low voltage, and our scopes are extremely complex because it is mostly technology. Sound systems, mass distribution to multiple TVs, card access, camera systems, networking and so on. On this project I probably had about 30 - 40 different scopes, alternates or VE (value engineering) options on my proposal.

I knew everyone. I knew how they would function, be installed, and I would train the staff. Do you think my competition would be as knowledgeable, as detailed and most importantly, prepared? Probably not.

What if I did not prepare?

Let's put it into a different perspective. Let's say you didn't prepare, and you know nothing about the project.

What do you think will happen? Do you think the owner would like you to know nothing about their million-dollar project? Do you think they would trust your team? If you can't handle the meeting to coordinate the project, how can you be trusted to coordinate the project once it starts?

Being prepared is a mindset

Okay, how about real estate? There are 1000's of realtors. So maybe one or two might read this book. And it never made sense to me until after I started my construction business.

Prepare for your home tour. I want you to know the best schools, how far away they are, is it in a flood zone, slab, or raised foundation, and what are the upgrades. And so on, and so on.

Be an expert on every home you show a potential buyer. Take 5 minutes before entering the home, look at your notes and be an expert to your buyer. Chances are you will sell more homes. Your presence will also transmit confidence because you're ready for anything and know the home inside and out.

I can't count the number of homes I showed and how I struggled to make a sale. I was never prepared, I thought people would just want to buy a home. I didn't stop and think that this is the one of the biggest purchases a person will make in their life. And the amount of pressure that puts on someone.

I also never related someone being prepared would translate to trust and confidence to the home buyer. Preparation will work for any field; you just need to learn how to prepare. For real estate it is the home you are showing, or the comparable homes in the area if you are having a sale.

For construction, you need to know the scope of work. Now, if you are new to meetings and preparation, then this is going to be on the job learning. The only way to get better is to fail, reflect, learn, and pivot.

You can prepare for more than one area of your business.

Here is another example. Let's say you're hiring an employee to join your company. With all the companies that are hiring, what do you think will set you apart from your competition and get you the workers you need? That's right, preparation, and confidence.

Prepare with questions about experience, rate of pay expected, and travel. Whatever questions you can think of in advance. Look at them throughout the day. Do they make sense, would you get enough info?

Would they be good questions? Take a minute and go on to some job boards. What are the qualifications and skills that the competition is looking for?

Then put the shoe on the other foot. Do I sound like a company I would want to go work for. When we first started, I was doing interviews and I had nothing to offer the employee. No vacation, paid holidays, or benefits.

My competition had all of the above plus some. Trucks, gas cards and retirement. Plus, they have deeper pockets, they can offer their potential employees more money.

If you were an employee and were looking at potential companies, what would be your deciding factor for doing the exact same type of work? It would probably be the perks I just mentioned.

How does a new company compete with a more established company? Taking the time to analyze every aspect of your business. Seeing where you can improve and taking steps in the right direction.

By becoming an established company, or at least appearing to be established, and offering some of the perks, like vacation or gas card, you can get quality employees to help you build your company.

It's tough

It is tough paying all those things when you don't get a paycheck yourself. We had to hire friends to get started, and I mentioned, we worked and filled in the gaps. But you need to have a goal to work towards.

We must sell our company to our employees just as much as they must sell themselves to us.

HR

Preparation comes in all shapes and sizes. One type of preparation is preparing for legal battles before they even start. Small businesses with employees that lack HR have a greater chance of being sued. People will look for companies without HR just to sue them.

It seems like we live in a sue happy country, and with more and more laws getting added to the books to protect employees, employers need to minimize risk.

Once we got to 5 employees, I knew we needed help, and I also knew we didn't have the budget for another office employee. We were barely getting paid at this point. I heard a commercial on the ED Mylett show, it was Bambee HR.

At the time it was $199 a month and the employee range you could have on staff was 5-20, if I remember correctly.

It has gone up to $299, but that is nothing to pay per month for up to 20 employees.

For a year we will spend $3,600 on HR. That is what, 3 weeks of pay for a full-time HR person would cost us?

You get to ask them all the questions you can think of. Question like, what not to ask in an interview, or can I send this email to every employee, or should I send the email individually?

You can also have them write custom policies, keep files on record and even do training.

In California, where I am from, there is so much red tape, you need to know what you're allowed to do and what not to do.

My partner didn't think it was worth it. Then he saw all the policies we made to protect us. Meal waiver, vacation, sick time, attendance, etc. We had unlimited policies when we first started. Now there is a cap, we can add 7 on top of our core policies. From what I can tell, we really don't need a policy until something happens in the company. We have only used 2 of the 7 policy credits over the last year.

Did you know in CA that it is mandatory for employees to take sexual harassment? I didn't until I asked my HR rep. HR is going to be your line of defense against being sues. Take the steps to prepare yourself and your company.

I also received a call from Bambee letting me know that 401K is now mandatory in CA as well. That just passed. We could be at risk without the help of our dedicated HR rep.

Conclusion

As you can see, preparation can land you jobs, protect your company, and help you build trust with your customers. Preparation is critical to anyone wanting to build a solid foundation for business.

I am curious what you think and how you would handle preparation for your company.

Where do you see yourself lacking preparation?

53

Chapter 5: Give it 1 More Day

I owe this chapter to Ed Mylett. I didn't want to take credit for this concept, but I did want to talk about how his book has helped me. Ed's book *"The Power of One More"*, talks about how he tells himself, to give it just one more day. Want to quit? Give it one more day. Had enough? Give it one more day.

Another concept I got from the book was, do you have a special someone, parent, or kid? Treat today like it's the last day you will see them. Because you never know when that might be. Don't take life for granted. Appreciate every second. And live in the moment.

Okay, so how did Ed's book help me? Well, when you are a business owner and you have employees, payroll, bills, materials, taxes, insurance, customers, deadlines, meetings and so on. It can be overwhelming. I have wanted to quit countless times. And all I say is just give it one more day. And 3 years later, we have a successful business.

Let me tell you a dirty little secret every successful entrepreneur knows. Starting and running your own business is the single most stressful, tiring thing you can do.

It is glamorized on social media and the web, but until you do it, you will never know what it's really like.

It will take everything you have to keep going. And all you need to do is take it one day at a time. As Tupac said, *"Through every dark night, there's a brighter day after that"*.

The moral of this chapter is to not give up. But you do have to know when to quit. It is a contradiction, I know. Let me explain.

If you start an online business and start selling products, you need to accept when a product isn't working, either cost, profit, marketing or whatever it might be. The power of one more does not mean to force anything. It is to stick with whatever you're doing if you think it truly has potential.

The power of one more is to not give up unless it is necessary. And you will know the difference. You will feel it in your gut. Like when I want to quit working at my company. I know if I give up, I could miss out on a business that has the potential to be a multi-million-dollar company.

I knew I had potential to grow a million-dollar company because I already have. And I did it for someone else. I knew deep down that I could do it again.

My mind says one thing and my gut/subconscious says another. I know deep down that after all my blood, sweat and tears, it will be the single worst decision in my life if I quit. So, I give it one more day. One more chance, one more attempt.

It is easier than ever to start a business

In modern times it is easier than ever to start a business. You can start an online store, order products, get a business license and start selling products. The structure of the business is a little different, but the potential is the same.

Let's say you start an online business; it costs you $250 to start. Took you a measly 16 hours of work to get the site up and running. You realize that you should have picked a more general name or need to change the layout of the site.

You don't need to stick with it if you are 100% convinced it will be unsuccessful. You can try something completely new.

Now, on the other hand, let's say that online business has been going strong for 2 years. And you hit a roadblock. No sales for months. Do you give up? No, change the ads, change the product, change the follow-up, change the discount. Pivot and figure out how to get back to where you were.

I started drop shipping an item I thought would do well. I made a site and started making some sales. But getting the item to the customer was becoming a nightmare. 2 months had gone by, and the item still didn't ship. Yikes! There is a flaw in the design, and I need to stop.

Looking back, I could have handled it differently. Yes, I could have bought in bulk and shipped directly to the customer when I got the order. But I did not believe this was my path. I took the lessons I learned from that business, and I applied it to my next business. It created a snowball effect.

With each business I brought a new skill, until in one business I had all the skills necessary to be successful.

3 years later

This book has taken me over a year to write. I have had many ups and downs. I am currently on my 3rd year of being in business. If I had listened to myself 2 years ago, I would not be at the current level of success. We have 6 full-time employees and 2 office staff, me, and the CEO. That is 8 people on payroll.

The potential for our company is endless. But you must go through the rough patches. Being an entrepreneur has ups and downs. If you weren't born into a wealthy family, chances are you either must do it all yourself or borrow a ton of money to get going.

Ask yourself, is this company worth it? Be honest, is it worth the time and effort? Is it worth the 50-60 hours a week of work.

Is it worth the nauseating stress that comes every day? Well, for me, becoming successful and eventually growing a company that can run itself is worth it for me.

I know if can be done. I know I can have a company that will eventually be able to grow without me.

Before you quiet, give it one more day, and see if tomorrow changes.

Conclusion

You will know in your gut if you should give up. If it isn't clear what you should do or you're on the fence, then give it one more day. But this book is not just about business. It is also about personal development.

In your life you need to make choices on when to dig in and when to give in. Go until you cannot go anymore.

Life will be tough, but each day you become a seasoned individual on a path of constant learning and evolution. Give it one more day and see what happens.

What is something you think you gave up too early on?

What do you think would have happened if you stuck with it just a little bit longer?

58

Chapter 6: Finding A Mentor

Have you ever heard the phrase by Pablo Picasso, "Good artists borrow, great artists, steal? I relate the quote to my business, and my business mentor. In a way I feel you are cutting the line and jumping ahead instead of trying to learn everything on your own.

Finding a mentor can greatly increase your chances of succeeding and also cut learning time in half.

Like the quote above, I think of it as stealing someone else's experience for my own benefit. Although we are not stealing, and chances are the mentor is willing.

I asked my mentor probably 1000 questions. This is a double edge sword. Because having the information available will cause you to not search out answers on your own. Which is something I have been learning.

A mentor can be anywhere and anyone. I have seen successful business owners have their dads as mentors, and I have also seen stepdads be mentors. If you don't have a good dad or stepdad to look up to, then you might find a mentor at work or maybe a coach.

I was not fortunate to have anyone in my life that is a entrepreneur. I didn't have a business owner in my family that I could turn to. Everything I learned I picked up outside of my home. I got lucky and met one of my mentors at work. He is a little rough around the edges, kind of old school, but he taught me a lot about running a company and how to make money. That experience is invaluable!

A lot of successful people have mentors. Here is a list of a few.

Tony Robbins - Jim Rohn
Warren Buffet - Benjamin Graham
Steve Jobs - Bill Campbell
Ed Mylett - Tony Robbins
Richard Branson - Sir Freddie Laker

The list above is some of the best of the best in business. And that is who you should copy if you want your business to survive.

That mentor I just mentioned, became my business partner. And yes, we are both stubborn, and we have our ups and downs like a married couple. But we made it through it. We can now both say we own and run a million-dollar business.

I look to him for guidance on products, purchasing, management, and countless other things. He brings a wealth of resources to our company that would take years to learn. He brings real-world experience that acquired when he ran his own business for 15 years.

Here is a tip if you are thinking of partnering with a mentor. Having a business mentor is a 2-way street. You need to bring something to the table; you cannot rely solely on the mentor. They will get burnt out on you and feel like they are carrying most of the weight. That will cause resentment and the company could fail.

I brought advertising, patience, and an unorthodox approach to getting business. Which has worked for us.

Bonus tip, never outshine the master. You can praise yourself, but remember, you would not be where you are without your mentor/partner.

Non-business mentor

Having a mentor, you look up to and get advice from is a little different. You don't share a bank account or must make payroll, lay people off, etc. There is no stress. Just talking and working through problems.

You don't need to bring anything to the table except a sponge to soak up all the wisdom.

Searching for a mentor

When you can't find a mentor in person it is safe to say that picking up a book or watching a video with a favorite business professional can get the job done.

I personally look up to 4 people that are on the mentor list.

Tony Robbins
Jim Rohn
Ed Mylett
Tony Robbins

I read their books, watch their videos and I even listen to their podcasts. You are who you hang around. I want to hang around the best, even if it is not in person, then it will be in my imagination, book, or video.

Honestly, I would not be where I am today if I did not have a mentor. I started a business with mine, and we are doing well to say the least.

Pick 3 people that you think can be mentors. If you have a mentor, who is it and why?

Can you think of anyone else that would be a good mentor?

Does this chapter make sense? If so, what did you learn from it?

63

Chapter 7: Who Are Your Competitors

Each chapter I write is so powerful. This chapter is just as powerful as any other chapter in this book. Who are the top 5 companies in your industry and in your area? Research your competition.

What are they charging, what products are they selling, and are they union? Who are the owners, or presidents, how many techs do they have, how does the office run, and what is the business location? Whatever field you're in, know your competition.

How many offices do they have, and what distributors do they use? Who are the customers, how do they get customers, and what certifications do they hold?

These are all questions I ask myself. I constantly check up on my competition.

Not only do I check up on my competition, but I also worked for them. I guess that is the benefit of being in the same industry for 15-20 years. Two of the companies were early in my career when I had little direction. I basically collected a paycheck, I never learned what made them successful. I eventually learned that a company I worked for was doing 20 million maybe more. That is a big player in our space.

I know the presidents and CEOs of 3 competitor companies. But that isn't enough. You need to deep dive into how they operate and why they are successful. How do they get business. What has made them so successful?

Where can you find out about them?

Their website will tell you a ton about their business strategy. Linked In, Facebook, Instagram. Whatever you can find out gives you an advantage.

You are competing with businesses that have been in business for 10, 20, 50, 60, or even 100+ years. How are you going to stand out from them?

These companies have a major pull and get projects handed to them. Or let's say it's a realtor that has been in the business for 20 years. They have a referral base like no other. They probably don't even advertise at that point. How do you compete with them? You learn!

For instance, I did real estate for a while, I was on some heavy-hitting teams in my area. What was one of the most important things I learned from each one? The *money* is in the *follow-up*!

I would have never seen that unless I joined their teams. Each one had a different approach but accomplished the same thing.

One had software to do the follow-up and one used the phone and a simple spread sheet. Now I can use what I learned from them on my own. The teams that I was on, are not my competitors and I sure did learn a lot!

E-commerce

Let's use another example, this can be for e-commerce, construction, and real estate. Heck, it can be for a ton of industries. I used this mostly in real estate and e-commerce. Since I already touched on real estate, I figured this would be a good example for e-com.

Facebook has a transparency page called *Ad Library*. Some might have heard of this, and some might use it. If you do use it, it is good for you. If you never heard of it, it is basically a place to see your competitor's ads on Facebook.

Here is the link https://www.facebook.com/ads/library/.

Now not all company ads will show. And that is because they use other companies to run ads. But anyone that makes their own ads will be easy to spy on them and see what they are doing. The longer the ad is running the better. People don't spend money on things that don't work.

You can't see what groups they target but you can see how they write the ads. Which is a huge advantage. Is it quick and to the point, do they include phone, email, and website links? How many images are they using? How long has the ad been running?

The point of this chapter is to spy on the competition and learn as much as you can about them. You can even go to work for them and learn the process and procedures. It will help a ton.

If you want to start a coffee shop, go work at Starbucks, even if it's only for a couple of weeks. Learn orders, inventory, and customer service.

What industry are you in and what competitors do you have?

Have you spied on your competition?

67

Chapter 8: Advertising and Marketing

This might be the longest chapter in the book. I have learned so much over the last 10 years. I have broken advertising and marketing down into different sections.

Paid Advertising
Organic Searches
Website
Business Page
Yelp
Landing pages
Duns and Bradley
Social Media Page

If you are just starting out, then I suggest paid advertising until you get your organic traffic going.

Now, before we get into the paid traffic, I know some start a business like Real Estate. And since Real Estate has a low financial barrier for entry, you might not have the funds to do paid advertising.

You might want to start doing open houses, or door-knocking. But paid advertising is worth its weight in gold and is the lifeblood of some businesses.

Paid advertising

Okay, pay to advertise. I recommend 2 platforms. Google and Facebook. Pinterest is a decent platform, but the audience needs to fit. You can also try LinkedIn and Tiktok. The thing to remember is, where are the people that you want to do business with?

Google is great for lead generation. Like Real Estate, construction, lawyers, or something similar. Anything that has high-profit margins. I have personally landed large contracts off Google ads.

Facebook is good for impulse buying. E-Commerce, or restaurants. Although things change constantly. Think about it, how many people go on social media before lunch? How many scroll all day and how many go out to eat?

And let's say they have seen an ad for a local restaurant. Buy one get one free! How many people do you think would be lining up at the door waiting to get a free meal with a friend? I bet quite a few. Another way to get business is to have local people post TikTok videos of your restaurant. I have seen countless times, videos with good-looking food attract customers bunches.

People are not going to know who you are unless you tell them. I watched the famous chef Gorden Ramsay grow a frenzy about kitchens he was trying to save. One of the shows, I think was Kitchen Nightmares, he would go around and get a bunch of people to fill the restaurant.

How? Passing out flyers, lunch specials, and he probably offered free food if the customers told their friends.

Offer a free meal to guests in the restaurant, then, and hopefully they will like the food. If the food is good, they will keep coming back.

Marketing is whatever works. When you find something, double down and prepare for what you need to do to handle the massive number of customers you will be helping.

We must turn off our marketing and go week to week. Why? Because our phone rings **TOO MUCH**! Yes, we get so many calls we stop answering and mainly respond to emails and voicemails.

Okay, this book is not how-to for advertising. It's to point you in the right direction. Give you some tips to get started. I recently watched a video that Mark Cuban did. He said that every business needs a salesperson, or they won't be in business.

Do you know why companies like Paul Mitchel are so successful? Because the founders were not afraid to sell. They knew the product in and out and they created a stir. They talked to the right people, hair salon experts, and convinced them that they needed to give the very best products to themselves and their customers.

Google ads

I am a master Google advertiser. And I will let you know a tip that can save you some serious cash. This tip not only will save you money, but it will help you get more targeted ads. What does that mean? It means that the people that call you will be interested in what your selling. Instead of using a shot gun approach which is gun shot with a lot of spread. You will have a laser shot, targeted at the right people.

This is the single most important area of your ad campaign other than your keywords and ad copy. It is basically a pie cut in 3 slices. The 3rd part is to **build your negative keyword list**. What a negative keyword list is, is it helps block people that might be looking and not ready to buy.

Types of keywords

We are all in business to make money. So I think it is safe to say that we do not want to give our products or services away for free. Well, if this fits your business model, the first negative keyword I would start with is free. By adding free to the negative keyword list, you add will not show when someone types free into the search bar.

Some other key words I like to add is cheap, how to, training, and so on.

Adding states is also a good one. Add the states that you do not work in. You can also do this with counties and cities. I feel this is a never-ending battle and should constantly be checked.

Watch it daily

Watch your add account daily. I ran 5 different campaigns for one of my companies.

What I learned was to try 5 different and unique campaigns. See what campaigns are eating up all the money and what ads are delivering quality leads. You can shut them off and run them one at a time. Or run them all at once.

I ran 2 at a time. I was running ads for cameras, and boy was that a bad idea. So many cameras' companies it is hard to exclude them all. I had to add 10 brands to my negative keyword list a day.

I ended up canceling it because it was just a waste of money. And no solid leads.

Words searched.

Constantly look at your words searched. This is usually on the home page of Google Ads. Look for keyword searches, click on the words, and look for an option to "add to negative keywords".

Google changes this layout all the time. The main thing to look for is what keywords your ad shows for. And click the words you do not want to show for. Then select the option to add to the negative keyword list.

When adding a negative keyword to the list, I like to add it as a ***broad term***. I find that the broad term is most helpful to stop my ad from showing to people I do not want it to show to. I also add it to the campaign, not the ad group. Adding negative words to the campaign will help when running different ad groups.

Research the competition

Here is another tip, like what you do with Facebook ads, you research your competitors. Do some Google searches and see what is getting used as the headline, aka hook, and what is in the text section. Are they using keywords, symbols, and so on?

Do they have a phone number showing links to pages. What is your competition doing and most importantly what are they spending money on.

Another pro tip, I try to keep my ad in the top 3 range. I find this gets me the most leads at the best cost. You can spend $.50 a click, or you can spend $50 a click. You better have a good landing page and follow-up if you're paying $50 a click.

If you have a good headline, you can still get good leads even if you're not at the top. Another thing I found was if you advertise and you only have 10 other companies in your space. You will show up twice, one for your ad and one for organic. If a person sees an ad, then another link with your name and you got some good reviews, you have a good shot at getting a call.

Landing pages

Landing pages are one of the single most powerful ways to drive traffic to your inbox. A high-converting ad is nothing without a high-converting page to land on.

There are a few books by Russell Brunson I suggest reading. He is the one that helped start Click Funnels. Click Funnels is basically a landing page builder that comes with a monthly cost.

The books are for a complete beginner, all the way to advanced. And will break down more about driving traffic to your site and how to convert leads into buyers.

Landing pages are a must, and they are simple. The main part is they need to flow. Image, info, call to action. Repeated, over and over on the page until your message resonates and they want to take action.

Different layouts but the concept remains. And a good hook, like a free trial, always helps.

If your business takes calls and emails, I recommend a banner with that contact info. Then the hook, then your contact info again, then a hook, maybe a sign-up, then contact info or sign-up sheet, and repeat.

Landing pages are all about split testing to see what coverts the best.

Look at sites next time you see an ad, what are they doing? How are they converting potential customers?

There is a ton of videos that explain how to do this. I recommend building a landing page specifically for a product. Although it will take time to get organic traffic, the page is there for years to come, and it takes a few hours to build.

I have done a few landing pages, and they rank on Google at some of the top spots. And I am also competing with the brands I am promoting.

Here is some more advice on landing pages. Be the first to write about a product and add a location. Chances are you will get some traffic.

There are a ton of videos on YouTube I recommend watching to see how a page should be designed.

Website vs social media page

This really depends on your budget. If you have the money to spend on a website, then do it. If you don't, a Facebook business page will work until you get some cash. Having a website is like owning a piece of digital real estate. The sooner you start it the better off you will be.

One of the things Google does when ranking websites, is it considers the age of the website. The higher the age the more trust Google will have.

WordPress is one of the easiest ways to build a site. Wix is also easy to use but I have always used WordPress. Unless I was making a store, then I would choose Etsy or Shopify.

If you get WordPress, I recommend Elementor. The paid version is about $50 a year and well worth every cent. A recent update lets you create pages even easier.

There are a ton of tutorials on how to build a home page. And you can download templates for Elementor when you get the paid version.

The best part is you don't need to do any coding unless you want to customize items to your liking. But I find everything I need can be done out of th box with Elementor.

What I like about WordPress is it has been around for a long time. At the time of writing these 810,000,000 sites use it. Plus, you get to use a ton of free plugins.

Anything from spam, caching, SEO, and so on. And there is no cap on the number of pages, posts, or menu items. You have complete control.

Hosting

Hosting is another thing to think about. I personally use Greengeeks. And have used them for 10 years at the time of writing this. They are a green company. I get shared hosting for my sites. It's cheaper and does what you need if you're just starting out. I would be a fool to wright a book and not put my affiliate link in it.

https://www.greengeeks.com/track/jrovito45/cp-default

It helps support all the content of this book and hopefully, most of all, helps you. Now if you are reading this book, I think it's safe to say you want to make some money. Then don't get mad, that is what affiliate marketing is about. I hope you will take this free advertising tip, and do it if you have the opportunity.

Back to hosting. I get a 3-year plans for $350. And a domain name (www.yourcompanynamehere.com) is about $14 a year. I think they recently changed that and now only do 1-year agreements.

I started a company https://www.omnisquared.com/ and made the site in a few hours with stock images from https://pixabay.com/. A lot of the images do not need to be credited to the owner. Make sure you check the copy written laws.

It doesn't matter who you get hosting from as long as they have a good deal on hosting, 99% uptime, and fast servers. Nothing like hosting a site and it doesn't load. I have seen a few.

When I check other sites I see some slow load times, so don't jump to get a site made until you look up who is doing it. I read a interesting fact a few years ago. Customer will leave the site quicker if it is hard to figure out. You have a matter of seconds to win over the customer or lost them. That would include load time.

Organic Traffic

When someone searches your business, for a specific keyword, you want your website to pop up. This is called organic traffic. It took us 1.5 years to start ranking consistently at the top of a Google page.

I own a construction company. And there are about 50direct competitors in my immediate area. Some have been around for 20+ years or so. Beating out those types of companies will be hard but not impossible.

The good thing about my competitors is they have outdated websites. Or they have errors. I still constantly check my competition and see what they are doing. The thing is, when you get an established company that has word of mouth, they don't care about SEO. They don't need it.

That leaves us to pick up the $50,000 crumbs they probably don't want any way.

You will want to focus on keywords older more established sites might not go for. For plumbing, it might be "trenchless". For a dentist, it might be "implants".

There are tons of books on SEO. And you can also take free classes. If you want to start generating free organic traffic, you are going to want to invest in this area of advertising and marketing. SEO is like the marathon of advertising.

Once you start ranking you will start getting free traffic. And free traffic that converts is literally priceless! In a previous chapter, I mentioned Yoast SEO. That will help do the basics. Although it looks like the free help has changed. And now the best option is paid. But books and videos will be a ton of help.

Another website is SEMrush, which will do an audit of your site for free. They can give you errors and explanation why your site might not rank.

You can publish your pages in a few different ways. Either submitting them to Google or having Google search your site randomly. I typically submit although I don't need to know. I made a page, searched the next day and it was published.

Backlinks are another great way to get your site noticed. A backlink is basically another site that links to yours. Like a Facebook post, or another blog leaving a link to your site in the post. This is another way you build trust with Google.

Business page

If you haven't published a Google business page, then you are missing out. It is a great way for potential customers to find you. You can add an about section, company photos, phone numbers, hours, and some items on how your business operates.

It is also a great way to get reviews. Google will let you share a link directly with customers for reviews. You can also add services that your company does. Like window washing, glass cleaning, high rise window washing. Whatever services you offer you will want to list.

My business gets searched 1000's times per month. Are all the searches relevant? No, but some are. And that is what counts. 1 call is all it takes.

You can use other search sites like Bing, but I don't get the amount of traffic like I do from Google. However, Bing is worth setting up a business page. If you get 1 lead a month or even a year, it is worth the few hours to set up.

Yelp

Yelp has its ups and downs. I have a few reviews on Yelp, and they don't show. Which is silly. And Yelp didn't drive the traffic I wanted. But it could work for you, and it's free to get started. You can also get promotions on ad credits. I suggest trying ads and seeing if it works.

If it doesn't generate the leads you want, cancel, and keep searching for what will work. Pro tip doesn't listen to everything the salesperson says. I was told that the site can generate my commercial leads, and that was a lie. They don't know what traffic is right for you. But it is worth experimenting.

I tried ads a few times, and neither time worked. We landed a few $250 leads, and for us, it isn't worth our time. There are other sites that you can run ads on. Sites will promise to generate leads for you, but it will come with a high cost. My suggestion is to master Google, YouTube, or a social media site.

If you're a Realtor, I know Zillow or Realtor.com offer leads, and I have converted a few. I know they work.

I always like giving advice, if you have some questions, reach out.

Email list

A no brainer, depending on your company, this should be a major focus. We don't really need it because we work with general contractors. And we do repeat business with about 10 companies. But for something like a restaurant or a bookstore, this will be a great place to blast coupons or promotions.

I really cannot express the importance of an email list. It is basically your own personal customer directory.

Duns and Bradstreet

This will vary for some businesses, but for us, we are constantly getting our business credit run. Duns and Bradstreet are like Credit Karma for commercials, or at least that is my understanding.

It also allows companies to find your company and see some statistics about you. When you apply for credit cards or a vendor does a check, chances are you will get an email notification from Duns and Bradstreet your credit has been ran.

Social Media Page

If you want to generate business then you will want a social media page, or maybe a page on every social media site.

With a social media page, you will obviously want to drive traffic with posts. The best sites I think are TikTok and Pinterest.
Instagram and Facebook are okay, but I don't have much success organically.
TikTok you can go viral as I mentioned earlier.

Play around and see what works. Some people recommend trying 1 or 2 sites at a time. Posting about 1-5 times a day to generate real traffic.

I do a post on Facebook and had a few leads, but nothing converted that I know of.

LinkedIn is also a large site and is considered social media in my opinion. Great way to build a professional network.

Everything takes time to build unless you have a viral video or product.

Give everything a try and be patient. Hope this chapter gave you some good ideas or pointed you in the right direction. As always, reach out if you have comments or questions.

What can you do to start advertising right now?

81

Chapter 9: Partnership and Skillset

In this chapter, I want to talk about partnerships and skillsets. This type of partnership is specifically for owning a company together. Not relationships with other companies. In today's world, it might be difficult to do everything yourself.

That is one of the reasons I partnered with one of my mentor/managers. We worked well together over the years, and we made a lot of money doing it. Well, I made the owner of our company a lot of money.

And when I wanted a raise, it was like pulling teeth. Not to mention all the other things that come with a micromanaging boss. Like looking over your shoulder or asking you what you're doing. Or my favorite, why are you smiling? I am smiling because I enjoy life.

Now, having a partner might not be for everyone. Some people don't like to share in the profits. Funny, I heard a video from Alex Hormozi the other day. He said, why would you want 100% of a limited business?

Why not want 20% of multiple businesses? When you partner with other people that have experience, capital, and connections, you are setting yourself up for success. Rather than trying to do it all your own.

Now, don't get me wrong, not all people are what they seem. And not every business will succeed. I worked side by side with my business partner for years before I thought about starting a business with him.

When it comes to choosing a partner, you want to be right, 1,000% right. Do not rush into something and not know who you're rushing into it with.

As I mentioned before, my business partner is an old-school work-until-your-bones-break, no-sick-days kind of guy. And why not, he was raised like that. Me, I am an expert marketer, web designer, and lead-generating machine. I also do the books for us.

We have a good partnership when it comes to bringing different skills to the table. Not to mention he trained me in my previous position. So, I also have some of his skill sets now.

The reason why I wanted to write this chapter is to get this point across, you don't need to do it by yourself.

But not every idea will work. One time I started a company with my girl and a close friend. Let's just say we didn't have the same viewpoints and we never really made it anywhere.

But if you think someone will be a good business partner, and you have worked with them in the past, you might want to consider giving it a shot.

Another tip for looking at a business partner is to look at their personality and see what flaws you can find. What will you and your partner butt heads about? Then multiply that by 10 and see if you can take it. If you think you will be okay, then your partnership might have a chance.

When you have 2 strong-minded people you are bound to have arguments. I had to learn to let things go. My business being successful is well worth every second.

Skillsets and why you should hire the best

Before I jump into this section, I want to let you know that this part might take some capital. But I think it is worth noting everything that I have learned about skillsets.

I worked for a large well-known company. Like all companies, there were pros and cons. Let's call the owner Ted for the sake of privacy. The one thing that stood out the most to me is how Ted grew to be one of the biggest companies in the area.

He did it through skillsets. He hired the best office people in his industry. And the payoff was huge! You might think, I don't want to pay this person x dollars. That is a lot of money. Instead of looking for the ROI, this person could generate.

For instance, let's say you pay a person $125,000 a year. Yes, $125,000 is a lot of money, for some. Now let's see what a rockstar person added to your business can do. My example is based on real-world experience, that I have seen firsthand.

On average an estimator can land a contract ranging from $500,000 - $5,000,000. Give or take, I have seen less, and I have seen more.

On average profit is 10-20% roughly. I have seen 5-50% and even more than 50%.

But let's be conservative with our numbers. Let's say 20% of a $5,000,000 dollar contract. That is $1,000,000 after all material and employees are paid. Who wouldn't want to hire the best when they can make profit and land contracts like that?

Now, that is only one project your $125,000 *salary estimator* can bring in. It can take anywhere from a few days to a few months to estimate the project.

Now, let's say, that estimator only brings in 3 $2,000,000 jobs. Let's say at 10% profit, which is more than reasonable.

10% of $2,000,000 is $200,000, profit! Times that by 3, and you just profited $600,000. Minus the $125,000 salary, you end up with a $475,000 gross profit.

This might be a little excessive for new companies since contracts will be smaller. The company I was at was over 10 years old when I was hired.

Some companies might have projects at the $200,000 price. But you should be able to knock a few of those out each year.

Don't get me wrong, you shouldn't take a loan out to pay employees more until you understand the job completely. Are you able to handle that type of project? Building and growing on a solid foundation is key to success for any employee.

If you don't know how to run a business and manage employees, you have a higher chance of failing. Go watch a few episodes of "**Bar Rescue**". But if you have the foundation and the relationships it might be time to hire.

Smaller companies do tend to run a little leaner. And can make a higher profit.

Owning a company is not all fun and games though. People want to sue, and employees, contractors, customers, and taxes make it extremely difficult to succeed. The stress is endless. But in my opinion, it is worth it with the right foundation and the right staff.

Hiring the wrong people

I have seen the most experienced owners' higher people that talk the talk but couldn't walk the walk. They abused the gas card, ran projects into the ground, quoted material incorrectly, and lost money. Just an all-around loss. On paper they might have looked good.

I look for people that have a good flowing resume. Relevant job experience and length of employment. Those are a few things to look at when searching through resumes.

Now another key takeaway here is some people lie. They say they can do a bunch of things and can bring all this money to the table with these connections, and they end up leaching off of you. Be on the lookout for those people.

Watch and make sure your employees are working to the best of their ability. Don't micromanage, nobody likes that. But look at the numbers, look at the contracts, look at the profit. If jobs are going over hours figure out why and cut the dead weight.

The most important trait of a new employee that I have found is honesty. If you have a honest employee that shows up every day and works hard. Take care of them.

Running a restaurant

Let's say you hire a manager at a restaurant. In my opinion, hiring a great manager that can be your eyes and ears when you are not around could be priceless.

Pay the manager a little more, and they will be happy to help. You hire a few people that can follow instructions and you hire a rockstar manager to oversee it.

What would be the opposite of this? Hire a manager, underpay them, overwork them, and you could possibly get poor results. Do you think the manager will care about the success of the business?

Employees need to believe they have a future or are working towards a common goal to be the most productive.

I can't stress how much you should take care of your employees. They are the backbone of your business.

If you have questions or I didn't elaborate enough, message me, and let's talk about your specific business and its needs.

If you had the capital, what position would you hire first and why?

88

Chapter 10: Capital VS Financing

This chapter might differ for a lot of people. When I chose to start my company, I made the decision to start it without taking a loan. Now, if you can make it on very little money for 6 months to a year, then that might be an option. It took us about 1.5 years to get a steady paycheck.

I would think of your worst-case scenario, then double it. Because that is possibly going to be your outcome.

Now, looking back, it was the best thing we could do. No large loan hanging over our heads. A lot of sleepless nights worrying about money, but now we are finally trending water. All our hard work is paying off.

Luckily, we have a company that we can run from our homes. Most of our work is new or existing construction done at the project site. Our technicians go out and do installations and we help from time to time. We also manage the job, material, meetings and so on.

It is a good business model. Our most expensive cost is employees and material. People want to get paid, and it is your duty to make sure your people and vendors are taken care of.

Would I do it any other way? No, I feel I am here at this point in my life for a reason.

What is the flip side of that? You need a large amount of capital to finance a restaurant or a dentist's office. What do you do? Well, if you have a good business model or a franchise, I think you have better chances of succeeding.

What makes franchises so successful is they have systems in place for everything. I am not a fan of McDonald's food, but everyone knows who they are.

So, I will use them in this example of why I think franchises are so successful. When you join McDonald's, you go through some type of orientation.

After that, you either learn cashier, food prep, or drive-through. Food prep is very simple and uses very easy-to-follow pictures. Toast the bun, add sauce, add meat, cheese, and so on. Want to fry potatoes? There are steps to take spelled out for minimal thinking.

When McDonald's makes a burger in California it tastes the same as in New York. They make it the same way across all locations in the US.

These processes help the company in a few ways. As I mentioned before, consistency, aka taste, speed, and accuracy, is done the same no matter where you ordered your food.

Another example I am familiar with is a pizza place. I have seen pictures where the employees see how to add the sauce, the cheese, and toppings.

Simple and bullet proof, for the most part.

Now if you're going to take a loan out and not choose a franchise, make sure you have as many processes in place as possible. This will help you greatly.

I know restaurant owners that have million-dollar loans, and they are close to paying them off. It can be done. And guess what, they were a franchise restaurant.

On the other hand, watch an episode of Bar Rescue or Kitchen Nightmares. There are usually the same issues in each episode because a restaurant is failing. And although the solution is simple, it might take capital to get you where you need.

For instance, when a restaurant fails, decor, food, cleanliness, and employees are the main issues. Changing the layout and furniture cost money. Hiring a chef cost money. Training employees, cost money. So to have a well-run restaurant will take more capital because you need more tools.

When you work from home you can take those funds and allocate them to an area of your business. If you want to own a successful business, study other successful businesses. Evaluate what your costs will be.

If you can save and avoid interest and the stress of making a monthly payment, it might help in the long run.

What I recommend is investing back in the company. Build your bank account up until you can make payroll for 6 months to a year and still collect a paycheck. Obviously, it is your company, and you can do what you want, but I recommend holding out from taking large chunks of profit away from your business as long as you can.

My Processes

Whenever I make a bid or order material, I always have checklists and cheat sheets. I have a list of items that are used on every job.

I get my counts, add them to the material sheet, and I also leave a section for notes. Like exclusions or adds. Usually, material that is not common.

Then transfer those numbers into accounting software and change the pricing for each product.

After pricing, I add the material counts once again into the labor software.

I get my labor total and add that to the material software.

Then I work on making sure my price is competitive, which is key to winning. At least in my opinion. You can also win by knowing a trade or skill not everyone knows.

I then fill out a proposal and send it to the customer. I do this every time for hundreds of birds. And it has been very successful for me.

What's right for you?

If you have a 300K buildout you might need a loan. It is going to depend on money saved, ROI, and gut feelings.

Obviously, this is not financial advice. You need to check with your financial advisor to get all the numbers worked out and do what makes sense for you. This is just my opinion and what I did.

Take care of your credit

I can't tell you how many times customers have run my credit. Take care of your credit and pay your bills on time. You will also need good credit to get approved for credit cards. Credit cards will help you make large purchases and give you some cushions until customers can pay you.

I wrote a book on getting out of debt. It's called "How To Save Money, Stay On A Budget And Get Out Of Debt". Look it up if you want some tips on saving money.

The best thing to do is to learn how to budget and live off less than you make. Invest back in the company, don't spend all your profit. Chances are you will need a large amount of capital to make it through until customers pay you.

You can also use credit cards for points. Just make sure you pay it off before you hit with interest.

Saving money is a mindset. Once you start to learn how to adjust your spending to spend less than you make you will be in a better place. Then saving money becomes routine.

What do you see when you start your business?

Do you have the capital, can you save the capital, or will you need a loan?

94

Chapter 11: Always Be Learning

Always learning is one of the most important chapters in this book. If you weren't blessed with the highest IQ or the richest family, then you will need to be an avid learner.

You will need to learn a lot of things and be able to retain them. You must first master your business. The best way to learn is to fail. Reflect and grow.

Whatever that is, car salesman, Realtor, restaurant owner, plumber, consultant, and so on. Once you master the basics, you must evolve.

For instance, I own a company, me and my partner have been doing this work for a combined 45+ years. Our business can be successful if we only do one type of work. But as technologies progress so must your business. We have taken on other crafts to build our skill set. Card access, CCTV, Audio Visual, and we are also currently studying for our alarm license.

We can make 5 times more money by learning other skills. And we can learn more if we have more time. We outsource a good amount of work to partner companies. The best part about our partner companies is they also refer work back to us.

Each one of the crafts mentioned goes hand and hand with the other. And take a lot of learning and failing before mastery.

By learning all the skill sets, we can provide the best solutions for our customers. Rather than a bunch of different companies.

I have seen this on a project, and nobody knows or cares what the other is doing. The result is poor execution, and the customer suffers.

As a salesperson and a business owner, you owe it to yourself to have as many possible streams as possible of income. And be able to provide the best service to your customers or clients.

Certifications

Certifications are a great way to get your foot in the door. But actually, doing the job is way harder. Anyone can pass a cert and still not know how to do something.

Certain certifications can be offered for free from vendors. I have 5 or 6 cents and my partner has 10 or more.

The bigger certifications that are harder to get will also help build trust with potential customers. And some certifications are required to do business.

Another way to get certifications is to have employees get them. Why study and take tests if others can do it for you?

This chapter is simple, always keep an open mind on what to do. Master the basics before you move into another skill, or like in the previous chapter, I mentioned you can hire someone.

Hiring the right people

I will keep this brief since we touched on it earlier. You can always hire people that are smarter and more knowledgeable than you are. This will keep you from getting overwhelmed and having to learn everything yourself.

For instance, HR, or accounting. Those are two positions you should know about but rely on other people to help guide you.

Unless that's what you want to focus on, then hire a salesperson.

The best part about owning a company is you can pick and choose what you want to do. But, remember this, in order to grow you will need help. If you don't want to grow, then stay solo. But your earning potential could possibly be capped.

What to learn?

Well, I am constantly learning about how to improve my speech, my work ethic, relationships, and attitude.

How to relax and be patient. Money is also a great skill to learn about. If you make a lot of it, you should know how to keep it.

What areas do you need more training in?

Chapter 12: Focus

This chapter is about focusing. Now, a lot of people will say this. But not everyone will give examples that make sense. And seeing as there are millions of people, my analogy might make sense to everyone as well.

I cannot count the number of times that I have been worried about work. We started the company with $0 in loans. Didn't receive a paycheck for months. Started the company during the 2021 pandemic.

We went from no work and stress. To have 5-10 jobs doing at the same time, and now we are at 5-10 jobs each, going at the same time.

I wanted to project myself into the future on how to solve our manpower problem. But what I learned; is you need to focus on one day at a time. Handle your schedule and your workload that day. Adjust if needed and on the next day focus on that day and being the most efficient and effective as you can.

I also think you should have your end goal in mind. For instance, my end goal is 7-10 company trucks, 15 or more field employees, 2 office staff not counting the owners, and an office with a warehouse, conference room, and office for each person.

It's good to have a destination, and you won't know what that destination is or how to get there if you can't say it out loud. If you don't know where you're going how will you know what direction to go in?

But daily tasks are the key to having a productive workday. When you get busy it can be easy to get overwhelmed. In that moment you must learn to prioritize. What is the smallest and easiest task to accomplish with the quickest deadline?

Obviously, if you have a contract to write and it takes you 3 days to finalize or go on a quick home tour, which one would you do? The quick home tour will keep work flowing in for tomorrow, but the contract will help the money flow in.

Then you get a call on a referral, they need an answer asap. It will take you about 45 minutes to complete. What task do you do first? There is no right or wrong answer because each person has different priorities.

What I would personally do first is the quick 45-minute task, followed by the home tour, and then the contract.

The contract will take 3 days, what is a few more hours? In the meantime, you help other clients/customers, and those tasks allow you to get more contracts.

Post-it notes

I love post-it notes! I write down each task or project that needs my attention. If I get a call and the post-it notes come out. Deadline, the post-it notes are ready.

Then I take each note and consolidate all the notes into a single post note. It looks something like this.

Bill XYZ
Call XYZ about a service call
Send XYZ an email
Pick up material for XYZ
Bid due for XYZ
Schedule XYZ project
Order XYZ project

I look at what task is most important, how long it will take, and the timeline given.

The book Atomic Habits, By James Clead, says to break down everything into smaller and smaller achievable tasks. It alleviates the overwhelming feeling you get. That is how you build skills. That is how you become faster and more efficient.

When you work from home it will be hard to stay focused. It will be hard to stay motivated. To get up every day and put in a solid 10-hour shift.

Multitasking is a myth

I have heard that multitasking is a myth and I believe it. You cannot do two things at once. Your brain thinks it is, but you're just jumping back and forth. Instead of trying to do multiple things, as I mentioned earlier. Focus on one thing, complete it, and move to the next.

Now the caveat to that is, maybe the thing you're doing is boring or you're burnt out on it. That is okay, in that instance, do a little at a time. Sometimes I do estimates and do several projects in a day or week. I must read and count. If I get burnt out, I order material or work on a design.

Although I like to take a break from it, I know that if I don't estimate then I don't have jobs to do. Without jobs, the money stops flowing.

I like to go into the field and do physical labor, or shop for the best price on materials. That helps me recharge and hit the birds head-on.

Now if you have never bid before, well let me tell you, it is a confusing and exhausting job. Nobody uses the same terms, details are left out, and you must guess. But if you guess wrong, it could cost the company money, so you really need to know what you're doing.

After 6 years, I have a good idea of what is needed, but when you do larger projects, it takes a lot out of you.

What can you do to improve your day and focus more?

Chapter 13: Don't force it

Don't force it, is also another powerful chapter. One every entrepreneur should know and understand. This rule goes for more than just business. It works in relationships, money, and exercise.

The concept behind it is if you try to force anything, like a square block through a round hole, you will only be met with resistance. Why? Because it's not meant to be.

The more you obsess over something the more it won't work. It is tough to move on, but this is a must. Not everything will work out the way you want it. You need to learn when enough is enough. I say this over and over. Fail and reflect, it builds character.

Now I am not saying give up. Here is an example, you are a salesperson, doesn't matter what you sell. Cars, insurance, or rice. When you get a potential customer listen to what they say.

If someone calls me to sell me a product and wants to know how much I pay. And if they can sell their product to me, oftentimes I hear them out. But I will say no, I have distributors that treat me well, why would I change?

When someone calls to sell us marketing packages or website issues, I quickly say NO. Hard no, not interested don't waste our time.

I know what I want, and I am not interested. But let's say I got an email from a restaurant. If the food was good and the deal is something I typically get, then I open the email.

Chances are I will use the coupon or deal as well.

I used the coupon example because I cannot think of a time, I got a random call and went with a service they provided.

Now some people can be converted over the phone. Some cannot. The main takeaway is if you get a hard no, don't waste time. Move on.

Door-to-door sales

Okay, here is a quick story of finding your nose to get to your yes. And not forcing it. When I was in my twenties or late teens, I had a job doing door-to-door sales.

I would go into business and try and sell items. Coloring books, watches, hats you name it we sold it. Sometimes I got called every name in the book. Get out of my store you bleep! But it didn't stop me, I could care less what anyone thought.

I will keep going until I meet a nice friendly person. I wouldn't force it and waste my time and energy. I wouldn't say things like, oh why not, you don't want to see, are you sure, here please buy something from me?

I would leave and move as fast as I could and not look back. Because I knew a yes was out there, I just needed to find it. When you finally find the nice person, that says "What do you have?". Well, let me show you, here is the best thing since sliced bread, (put it in their hands).

The best part is the price! What's the price? The price is these sells in the stores for $20 bucks! I got them for $5! That's a good deal, right?

In sales, you cannot get discouraged and force it. You will quit and find something else.

Easygoing and relatable is what you want. Did you see the Knicks game last night? No, I missed it what happened? People want to do business with people they like. Not pushy salespeople. You won't win every battle. It is tough to let things go. I still get hung up on bids I lose. But rather than dwell, I try and improve.

When you feel yourself forcing something, take a step back. Relax, remember this rule, and pivot.

Meeting a millionaire

Have you ever shaken a millionaire's hand? When you shake a millionaire's hand, you feel a certain energy. This person understands how to attract money. They figured it out. Do you think they force anything? Or do they know their business, what they need to do, and execute it perfectly?

Another way to think about the don't force it rule, is in relationships. Let relationships evolve naturally. Don't force it. Most people at some point in their lives have liked a person or even loved a person more than the other has loved or liked them.

But sometimes we try to force the relationship. Because we want it. And what happens? The relationship is eventually lopsided and fails.

I have contractors that I work with and never won a job from. What was the issue? Them or me? Me, 100%, I tried to force it, bid everything I could, and never won. Why? Well, I asked a friend that was also a contractor. I asked, does winning come down to price and nothing else? He said, "Yes". Wow, I was shocked.

Do you mean even if they miss stuff, it's only about money? He said yes. Now, if the company sucks and they constantly miss stuff it will come out eventually.

But once I learned that it was all about money, my perspective started to change. How do I offer the contractor my best number each time and give our company a shot at winning?

I reflected and pivoted. I didn't try to force it and continue what I was doing.

What do you force and how can you fix it?

107

Chapter 14: Get Comfortable with the Uncomfortable

Most of you have heard something along the lines of getting comfortable with the uncomfortable. And it couldn't be more accurate. When in business for yourself, you will be met with challenges that seem impossible. Meeting prospects and being able to convert them into customers. Or fear of failing so you're not going to even try.

Cold-calling companies and pitching a script, facing rejection after rejection.

Whatever you're uncomfortable with, figure out why and how to overcome the fear.

Here is an example of a fear that I had to overcome. In the technological world, there are constant changes. Literally every time I turn around there is a new technology, access control, CCTV, alarm, and so on.

When you first start out you probably won't know the answers to customer questions. And that's okay. With each failure, you develop a layer of learning like non-others.

I personally learn through repetition. I need to learn, see, touch, and do something over and over before I get the hang of it. But once I do learn a new skill or technology, I become the most knowledgeable person in the room.

Power of belief

Knowing your products will help you overcome fear and boost your confidence. I know first time Realtors that killed it and sold a house the first week. Or someone sells 10 policies overnight there first week.

They believe in themselves. They act like they know it all when they don't know anything. They believe they are meant to help this person and they do.

When I went into meetings I would get asked questions about the process, or equipment, and rarely did I have the answer. I would constantly reference my partner, and at that time he was my boss. I would say things like "I'm not sure, let me ask". Or I would bring my then-boss and now partner in on every meeting, job walk, or phone call.

I feared not knowing the answer. All that would do is force me to stay in a comfort bubble. And my customers could see I didn't know as much as I should of. I lost trust.

It was my crutch. When I finally realized that this approach was hurting my business, I started to go out on my own. I felt differently. I talked differently, had more confidence, and knew I could serve my customer just as well as anyone else could.

My mindset shifted with one of the hardest things I had to do, sell myself and my products. Now when I am heading into a meeting, I still get nervous before the meeting starts, but the nervousness goes away as soon as I meet the customer.

When I won my first job with a well-known contractor. The project manager wanted to have a call and talk about the project. I reacted as I usually would and called my partner in just in case, I couldn't answer the questions.

The contractor expressed several times I did not need to bring anyone else in. It is a quick call. But me lacking the confidence, and just starting a business, I didn't want to say the wrong thing. So, I set up the conference call. What do you know that job went on permanent hold, or that was what I was told.

Either way, it was a lesson well learned. And that lesson was, it's okay not to have the answer, and I needed to fail on my own until I got it right.

With each call I took, and job I walked with a potential customer, I built confidence. Over the years I say something dumb occasionally, and I head to my car and say never say that again when on a job walk.

Now, when I talk it comes naturally to say the right thing. Repetition and failure. That is what compacts the foundation. You can't build on loose soil.

Making payroll and billing customers

Another uncomfortable experience was the billing. I would always wait for the bill. Why? I didn't want the contractor or customer to think I needed the money. But in order to have a successful business and pay my bills and employees on time I would need to overcome this fear.

Now, I ask for 50% down on small projects I go directly with the customer. On larger projects, I bill 20% for mobilization a month ahead.

When you break free and step out of your shell you can really shine. Turn that negative energy into a positive experience and you will eventually succeed. It is natural to get nervous. It is how you snap out of it that matters most.

What are some problematic parts of your business?

What do you need to do to overcome them?

111

Chapter 15: Rock Bottoms, Bottom

There are going to be times in a person's life when they feel like they hit rock bottom, and a few years later, it feels like they went even deeper.

My rock bottoms, bottom: this is such an important topic. Each law is going to be lower than the one before. On your entrepreneurial journey, you are going to have many ups and downs. But you will never hit bottom like you did before. It will always get deeper.

The best way to describe it is when you have the knowledge and skill, it makes you heavier. And you fall farther down the hole. At least that is my opinion. I think it is because I knew I could do better.

I am not sure how many people have had a similar experience. I am not sure if this is an income class issue or an upbringing issue. The book Outliers by Malcolm Gladwell says a few things about a child's upbringing and how it can give insight into a person's behavior.

A person that is more well off is encouraged to try new things without the thought of failure.

While the less well of person will be constantly said no, I can't afford it, or something like that.

Do more well-off people have rock bottom? I know when drugs are involved this could be true. A-list actors or athletes hit rock bottom.

The top of my rock bottom

This book has taken me over a year to write and edit. After a certain point of success, and failure strikes again, I feel like I hit the bottom of my top. With each new contract I go higher and higher. But with each rejection I only fall a few feet now.

And it is easier for me to bounce back. In the beginning I would fall and want to give up. Now I know what is possible, so it is easier for me to snap back. And not take it personal. Part of your journey is about learning.

Brighter days are ahead

What I do know is that with every low comes a high. When you hit the lowest point possible and want to give up, and nothing is going right, think of this book and know it WILL get better. It will be a matter of time, but time does heal the pain.

Not a lot of my friends would consider meditation. For me, meditation is the clearing of the mind. A re-focusing of my energy. Relaxation of the mind and body. Knowing I have been through worse, I only need to catch my breath and move forward. Center and re-focus on my goals.

Even when I am having a bad day, and can't snap out of it, I do a quick meditation. I say my affirmations, I know, I can, I will. And take deep breaths. I regain a sense of clarity.

I can't tell you the number of times I wanted to give up. Did I make the right decisions, is this the right industry, the right partner? And maybe if I didn't win a contract, my sales would instantly deflated.

But what I realized is, I can handle the bottom differently than I did in my previous years.

Have you hit rock bottom? If so, how did you get out?

115

Chapter 16: Ask for Feedback

Asking for feedback is a critical part of any business. How are you going to learn what you could do better without feedback from your customers?

Large companies do this every day. Let's say you don't have a sale. Ask the prospect why they made the choice they made and how you can improve. It's that simple.

Not everyone will respond. But when you do get a response, it will be an eye-opening experience.

For instance, I asked a customer that I had sent a lot of bids to. And I didn't win anything. I was puzzled. What am I doing wrong?

I asked why I didn't win and what I could do to get better. The answer I got was not what I thought. Many of the jobs bid on were not won by the contractor I bid to. Or I got slightly beat out in price.

What does that let me know? What do you think it helps with?

What do I think I got from the conversation. I learned that I need to reach out to more general contractors. Try to get my number in more contractor hands.

I learned that I need to tighten my price, mainly labor. And I would start to win the numbers game.

I also learned that not everyone wins all the jobs. Once you learn, continue to learn, and give it your best shot day in and day out, chances are you will succeed. We get seasoned. The reason why the pros succeed is because they put the reps in day after day.

Ask, and you shall receive.

Think of how powerful this is. If I was a restaurant owner and I was wondering why business was slow, I would ask customers what they thought of their experience. How was the food, atmosphere, service, and so on? I see Gordan Ramsey do this in Hell's Kitchen all the time.

This can tell you a lot of things. One of the most beneficial is what you need to improve on. What are your strengths, and what are your weaknesses? Don't be a business owner that is in denial. If people aren't showing up it is probably because your food sucks, your staff is rude, or your decor is dated.

But be careful when you ask people for feedback. For one, they could be having a bad day. Or their taste is a bit off from the norm. If you are serving a ton of people, get as much feedback as you can before you start to make changes.

That is why I suggest if you run a restaurant, get a few reviews before you make a change. If 9/10 people say the food was bland, well then it could be. If 7/10 says the decor is dated, consider the update.

Now if 1/10 people say you should serve ghost peppers on the pizza, do you think it is a good idea? Maybe, maybe not.

When asking for feedback depending upon the service or industry, you might ask differently.

An e-commerce store most likely will send emails. If you were a restaurant, I would walk around and ask how the food and visit was. Give coupons or a discount to people that leave feedback.

What feedback questions could you ask that can help improve your business?

119

Chapter 17: Does the plant have sunlight? Eliminate distractions to be more efficient.

This chapter is about paying attention to the little things. I can't remember where I heard this from, but it makes sense. If you must constantly divert your attention away from your company, your company will suffer.

I use the analogy of the plant needing sun because this recently happened to me. I have a cat that likes to eat my plants and make a mess.

To avoid the plant dying, I needed to move the plant to another room. Our house has a lot of shade. And most plants can't survive in a shaded room. Opening the blinds each day and closing the blinds each day was a task I had to do. The plant needs its sun. Or it would die.

Instead of leaving the plant in my kitchen with minimal sunlight and opening/closing the blinds each day. I went to the hardware store, got a plant barrel, and chicken wire, and made a new outdoor home for my plant.

Each day the plant gets light without me worrying or taking my focus away from my business.

The main takeaway from this is, even the slightest obstacle can drain you and take your focus away. One of Japan's oldest companies said what was one of the keys to maintaining success all these years. One of the answers was to not slow down. When you build momentum keep it going. Don't stop.

Well, being an entrepreneur where everything falls on you. And if you don't work you don't eat, it is critical for you to not let even the tiniest pebble slow you down. Now, the plant needing sunlight day after day may not be a big deal by itself. But if you have multiple items that constantly distract you, you will not operate at maximum capacity. You won't gain the momentum you need to get started and be successful.

Remove these obstacles from your life the best you can. Make your life easier, easier to focus on the things that matter. Like running and growing your business.

Remove the distractions, video games, social media, friends, at least while you're on the clock.

Keep your desk clean

Another topic I want to talk about is keeping your desk clean. When you have clutter you can feel overwhelmed. Eliminate that feeling by keeping your desk clean.

If the desk is too small, you might need to get a bigger desk. I got a 6' x 4' desk from Staples for under $200. I like to have space and not feel cramped when I look at my monitors.

I used double-sided velcro to keep my keyboard, mouse wrist cushion, and mouse pad in one place. I raised my monitors off my desk using monitor stands.

I try to keep my desk as organized as possible and in return, it helps me be more productive. Everything on my desk has a purpose. And if paperwork is on my desk, then that needs to get my attention first thing.

Take care of the little things so you can have more clarity to take care of the big things. Like growing your business to be a million-dollar business.

What are some distractions you can remove from your life right now?

122

Chapter 18: Brainstorming what you want to start

Most entrepreneurs that I have heard of do not come from well-off homes. They worked their way to the top by doing basic things and doing them better than anyone else. They are a, master in their craft.

Now, unless you're a savant, you are probably going to fail a few times.

In fact, there are a ton of things to try. Before I got started with my current company, I wanted to do computer networking. I like programming as a hobby, but I didn't want it as a job. Sitting in a cubicle and clocking in an out was not my cup of tea.

I tried tech support, fun, but not for me. Worked in a data center for years, good job but no future. Unless you wanted to kiss butt to get somewhere.

If you're trying to think of things to do to get started as an entrepreneur, consider doing a brainstorming session. Take a piece of paper, and a pencil or pen. Draw some circles. In each circle add a topic. Like, *businesses I want to start. What wakes me up in the morning?*

Maybe *working from home* is what you want. Put it in a circle and draw a line for each business you can think of that lets you work from home.

Here are a couple of examples to get started.

Insurance
Courses
E-book
3D printing

Accounting
Tax Preparation
Web design
App development
Construction
Vending machines
Shared office space
Delivery company
Handy person
Painter
Landscaper
Consultant
Junk removal
Mechanic
Cell phone repair
Truck Driving
Translator
Barber shop
Tow truck driver

Once you get some business Ideas you would consider, get another sheet of paper out. Add a few more circles. Think of how they would generate business. What certification or license is needed?

What is the cost to start the company? Let's look at tow truck drivers. I always wanted to start a company like this.

But came to the decision that tow truck driving was not for me. I would have to sit in traffic and pick up cars. Or I could hire someone, but I would need the capital to get going. Who are the big players in my area.

How many cars break down each year? Who would I need to partner with to get the business going?

When I looked at trucks a while ago, they were around $75K for a used truck. What else would I need?

A shop possibly or tow to a mechanic. Pay an employee for nights and weekends. Be on call. Insurance, maybe an A or B driver's license if you live in CA.

And hopefully some experience in this field. I drove a medical box truck for a few years. I have been behind the wheel of a vehicle for over 8 hours a day. A tow truck driver wouldn't be much different in my opinion. But I could be wrong.

Put the idea of what to look for in the back of your head. You will know when the opportunity presents itself. The best thing is to start and see what you want. Things change, what you want today might not be what you want tomorrow.

The business I chose I have been doing some form of it over the past 20 years. I knew what needed to get done to start it.

But as an alternate option to generate money, I wrote a book. I started a YouTube channel that I am going to get more serious about after this book is published.

I want to design simple t shirts for entrepreneurs. These are great ideas but if I was starting a service-based business and needed to get going. I might start painting. You can make a lot of money if you're good at it.

Don't listen to anyone but yourself (and maybe your spouse)

Chances are you are not going to be perfect when starting a business. If you believe deep down that you can succeed, then go for it. If you have a long-term committed partner, I will say to consult with them as well.

The last thing you want to do is put strain on a relationship. If you feel like your making the right move, let them know. If they are supportive, then they will support you.

The point I want to get across with this section is if you feel it in your gut, give it a try. Fail, pivot, and try again. You become successful by not giving up.

What business do you want to start? And why?

How much experience do you have in the business you want to start?

127

Chapter 19: Should you fire your bad customers

There will come a time in your company when you need to fire your bad customers. When you finally get going this will make sense, but when you first start out, it probably doesn't seem logical.

When we first started, we took anything we could get. Including a $225 residential cable job. Or hanging a TV for $125. Looking back, we were desperate. Now we have jobs that are in the hundreds of thousands. But we did not get to where we are by giving up. You need to stay consistent, stay resilient, stay motivated.

At the time, it made sense because I had $0 coming in. When you have $0 and not getting a paycheck you tend to take what you can get. One thing that helped me along the way, and I think I am going to start making, is, t shirts. I made a shirt that said "Don't quit". I would put this shirt on when I got discouraged. And it made me think to myself, don't quit.

Maybe I will come out with a line of shirts just for entrepreneurs. Shirts that nobody else would want or understand but us.

Okay, back to the whole fire your customer thing.

I tried to keep the small stuff going but was overwhelmed by my bigger customers doing larger projects. When you must manage, order, do sales, billing, and so on, it can be overwhelming.

After our second year, I had about 4 companies that needed our help when they had work in our area. I would help when they called. We had to drive all around town for a few hundred dollars. We finally got to a point where it did not make sense to continue the relationship.

And when they called, I politely told them we are not doing service work anymore. If they had bigger projects, we would be more than happy to help.

Don't get me wrong, the jobs were profitable, it was T&M, which is time and material. I billed from when I left my house to when I got home. But it was exhausting trying to keep up with the little things.

Our bread and butter have been having 2 techs on site for a few months. Get material here and there and do those 4 or 5 times. Way better than trying to manage 4 small projects a day.

Not only that, but I would also have to go do the jobs myself. Often, I would get random calls that needed a quick turnaround time.

I can't call technicians at midday and ask them to drive around town to do a job that we know very little about. Typically, the jobs had few details and you had to figure out what to do as you went. On top of that the techs would be driving their vehicle. Asking a person to drive their vehicle to several stops could drive your employees away.

We would reimburse as needed to stay compliant but figured it was best not to ask them, Also, the type of work was painful, you were by yourself, you have to deal with dirty ceilings and insulation, and it was all-around unpleasant work. Like the, watering the plant analogy, it drains you and takes away from other larger projects.

Now there are a few things to consider when you fire your bad customers.

#1 Do you have money coming in?
#2 Do you have potential money coming in?
#3 Will these small jobs lead to big jobs?

If it doesn't make sense, you will know and your gut will argue with your brain because you're turning down money. And that is fine, hold out until you cannot take it anymore.

But when you start doing larger contracts with bigger customers you will want to be 100% on top of your job. Not worried about small jobs.

We had a customer that started small, maybe a helper for a day. Then it grew to small projects ranging from $1,000 - $10,000. But they do mix in a few hundred-dollar jobs over the year.

I kept this customer. It makes sense, we make a profit, and they hand us work. But I did stop going out of town for them, now we only do local work. When you become successful you can make decisions in your favor.

Service based business

I want to give another example, not just construction.

This can go for Real Estate and any service-based business. But let's say you have a cleaning company. And your average account is $260 per cleaning which is about $65 an hour for 4 hours. You could land office buildings, but I will keep it simple for this example.

What would be a small job? Let's say a 1-hour cleaning is probably a small job. On top of that homeowners want to get a good deal and can haggle with you for a better price.

Again, if you have nothing coming in and no hope of anything coming in as well, then take what you can, so you can eat and pay your bills. But when you hit a point in your company where you are consistently bringing in larger amounts of money per job you might want to consider losing the 1-hour customers.

For instance, you have to pay for gas, supplies, and labor. By the time you or an employee shows up to work for an hour, how much are you going to profit?

To some it might be worth it, for me, I would try to get to higher price points and make more money on larger cleaning jobs. I know a lot of state agencies hire cleaning crews to work nights. Maybe 2 or 3 office buildings a night and you can keep a few people busy. And it is steady work. Offices usually want cleaning crews every night.

Real Estate

I was showing a property to a client a few years back. I spent weeks trying to get something going and nothing ever happened. I wasted all my time working on a large deal when I knew the person had no skin in the game. No skin in the game is a way of saying they have no money.

We were working on a 1.5-million-dollar deal. They had a few other properties that were owned by their LLC. The person was high up in the LLC so it gave me some confidence that things could go through.

But after a few contracts and a few backouts, my sales got deflated. I realized it was a waste of time and fired them. Best thing I could have done.

I always try to treat each customer or client the same. With respect, honesty, and integrity. And there is nothing wrong with that. But if they are causing more harm than good, it might be time to let them go.

I spent a lot of time chasing clients that were never going to buy with me. Or showing homes with the fear of not closing.

This tip might not be for new entrepreneurs because when you start out you will take anything. I was probably 2+ years in when I started turning down customers left and right.

We get calls daily and I still turn them down.

Does it make sense to fire smaller customers that have an increased difficulty with a smaller return?

133

Chapter 20: Taking care of your employees

Okay, I say this a lot, this is an important chapter. Well, this one is equally important as any other chapter. Unless you don't want employees. Then this chapter might not mean much to you. If you want to go solo that is perfectly fine. Some people want that.

Now, on the other hand, if you do want employees, then congratulations. You want to leverage your time by hiring other people to do work for you. The only issue with hiring employees is they cost money. The more experience the employee had the more they cost.

Employees are by far our biggest expense. But the beauty of a well-rounded employee in a service based business is if you can keep them working steady those are all billable hours.

I want to point out two examples to show a contrast between my thoughts on employees.

Example 1

You can treat an employee like they don't matter, try to take advantage of them, and constantly expect more. If you were an employee and you were treated like this, how hard would you work? Really hard, or not hard at all?

Probably not hard at all. Why? Because you are constantly told or shown that you don't matter. That you're just a person doing a job and you're not cared about.

You can also not pay employees fairly or give them raises. Complain when they take days off and basically treat them as if they are not human.

Example 2

Let's flip this. Okay, you have an employee, you praise them when they do well, and you take them out to lunch. You give them half days every so often when they do well and encourage them to take their vacation days. You give yearly bonuses so they can give a little something extra to themselves and their family during the holidays.

You try to understand the frustration and issues they face and do everything in your power to make life as smooth as possible. To listen and not place blame.

Do you think that employees will work harder? Do you think they will care every day they come to work? Will the employee feel appreciated?

2 types of people in this world

There are two types of people in this world. I am broadly generalizing in this example. An employer, and an employee. Not everyone thinks like an entrepreneur. Not everyone wants to work for themselves. Not everyone wants to have unlimited earning potential.

Employees want to go to work, make a little bit of money, and enjoy life. There are some high earners that can afford more and have better toys. Patrick Bet-David says they are *intrapreneurs*. People that want to help a part of a company grow and not actually own the company.

To leverage your time, you need to hire employees. Employees will make you rich. Remember that, write it down. Employees will make you rich.

There are some rules to that. The person needs to have skill and be productive. You can't hire 20 unskilled and untrained people and have them make you a millionaire.

Let's say you have 1 employee. That person on average generates $25 per hour profit when they work. $25 x 40 = $1,000. That is a $1,000 profit per week.

Okay, what if we have 10 employees? We make $10,000 a week profit. That is after taxes, expenses, and materials are paid for. And of course, if the employee is productive and well-trained. With 10 full-time employees in a service-based business you can generate $30-40K per month.

Once you hit 10 employees you must do things a little differently. At least in my home state California. OSHA, additional training, and a few other things come when you hit 10 employees.

Do you see the power of leveraging an employee? If you are a single person working, you are capped by time. That is why most people that work a 9-5 never get rich.

Now, running 10 employees is another story. To manage employees, you need managers. I will get to over seeing people in a second. But before I do I want to talk about taking care of your employees again.

And I think from the example, you can see how much a potential hardworking employee can generate per week.

Why would you not want to take care of that person?

Because you get greedy. We all do at some point. But you must let go of a little to get a lot in return. Understand that you are nothing without your employees. The earlier you accept that the better.

Now when you build your company you can create flourishing culture. Rather than a dreadful one. I know, I have experienced both cultures.

I have had the look from an owner, followed by why are you smiling? I avoided talking with that owner every chance I got. And I loved my job. Coming in working on numbers and counts. Trying to save as much money as possible while trying to maximize profits and employee output.

At the start of my 3rd year as an estimator, we were going to make close to $3,000,000 in gross sales. When I started, we were at $1,200,000 or somewhere around there. We more than doubled our division. Do you think it was luck? Or because we ran the division well.

We were not taken care of, mentally or financially. We dreaded showing up each day.

Take care of the people that make you money. Treat them well. And not for a selfish reason. Do it because you want to bring joy and stability to people's lives.

Hiring a manager

We are not at this point, but it is getting close. When you have too much work, and a lot of employees, you need to hire a manager to help. Someone to help when you are not present. Your manager must be someone you trust wholeheartedly.

It is impossible for you to run sales, manage the employees, make the orders, and keep taking care of your customers. You don't have enough time and your customers won't have the patients.

We are lucky we have skilled journeymen that have been doing the same job for years. They know what they are doing, and we trust them to get the job done when no one is looking. Eventually when we get too big, which is right around the corner. We are going to need someone to take over part of our workflow.

Take equipment lists, deliver material, attend meetings, and print plans. This person is going to oversee the entire operation. When I worked for a large electrical company, I learned a thing or two about structuring a company for success.

This is how it broke down.

Owner
Accounting
HR
Field Superintendent
Manpower Superintendent
Estimators
Project engineers
Safety coordinator
CAD designers
Warehouse manager
Delivery driver
Project managers
Project foreman
Apprentices

As you can see, that is a hefty payroll. But with that hefty payroll comes accountability. Each person has a specific role in the company. The owner has built a support structure like none other.

Now this is not just the company I worked for. This goes for any large successful company. You need the right support structure for your company to grow and take care of your customers. The owner did not get this way by accident. They were strategic in everything they did. From building relationships to completing projects.

But one of the things that he did best was take care of the employees. We had picnics, Christmas parties, bonuses, and company lunches. We got to leave early on holidays and got additional checks on our birthdays.

We might not have got along, but I respected him. And I knew I had to soak up as much as I could from him.

Do you think it is worth it to take care of your employees?

Do you even want employees?

140

Chapter 21: Taking care of the customer

We talked about taking care of employees, now let's talk about taking care of the customer. You will have many customers in your life. I feel you should treat each one to the best of your ability. Be honest, you're not going to get rich on one sale. You get rich by having a lifetime of sales.

Don't be afraid to tell customers what they need. For instance, I had a customer, a head IT manager for a very large company. We were on a job walk, and I let him know that he needed a certain part, or the system wouldn't work. I got a call a few weeks later. We won the job!

And why do you think we won the job? He mentioned while I was on site installing the equipment that he went with my company because nobody else told him he needed additional equipment. I didn't really think too much of it when I was telling him. After he told me what happened I really started to think about how I could do this more often.

It is like saying the wrong thing and how I must train myself to be selective in my wording. The same goes for helping, you must put your knowledge out there for people to see. Chances are you can land a contract or two.

We have done 7 projects over the last year alone. I also enjoy working with this person and don't mind going the extra mile or picking up things that we didn't have covered because I genuinely like him.

I think you should always take care of your customers, that is the point of this chapter. But you will develop working relationships that are a joy to be a part of.

Making friends in high places

I also have a quick story of a person that I have with over the years. This person doesn't have to give me the time to say, but he comes off as one of the coolest people I know or have worked with.

When we started, I tried to work with his company, and they gave us a shot, but nothing ever happened. Until about 3 years later. Yes, customer relationships can take a long time to develop. But if you stick with it, it will be worth it.

Once there is mutual trust built, watch out. We have landed several large contracts over a few-month period. The best part is we enjoy working with each one at their company. They are nice, professional, and responsive. Those types of traits in a company do not come around too often.

I met this person at my old company, he must have seen me as a nervous kid. And I was, the company made hundreds of millions of dollars each year. This was the big leagues. And now, I was able to bring that relationship to my company.

I can't tell you how blessed we are to work with them. And the reason why I am telling you this is because you must believe in yourself and your ability to take care of your customers. It takes time and patience.

What customers would you like to work with?

What customers do you think will be the toughest to land?

143

Chapter 22: The Why

Many entrepreneur books talk about your why. And why finding your way matters so much. It couldn't be truer, and I felt that it should be included in this book as well. Since the why is going to help you throughout your journey.

Why are you making the sacrifices, the long hours, the sleepless nights, the financial burden, the constant skill-building, and the extreme stress you will endure?

Take a piece of paper and write down what it is that motivates you to be your own boss. What are you doing this for? Is it financial freedom, spending more time with the kids, better pay, taking care of a loved one? Or how about better working conditions and less traffic? The flexibility to build your schedule the way you want.

Heck, those are all the reasons I made the leap. I sometimes think about working for someone and what it would be like. And it makes me cringe knowing I would have a boss to answer to. And I would have to punch a time clock.

Whatever your reason is, take a second right now and write out your why. If you cannot think of anything just start writing, more things will come. Get the creative juices flowing.

More money? More Freedom? More time?

The reasons I mentioned above are all made possible when you become an entrepreneur. Not many positions offer that type of freedom of choice.

Another goal of mine is to make more money to buy a piece of land. Have a place to retire or to vacation when I want. A place where the family can come out and camp, maybe build a cabin. And be able to leave it to the kids one day. And their families and kids can enjoy it.

Maybe you're wondering why generational wealth is. Whatever it is, find it, and use it to motivate you.

Things change

Yes, things change. Your why 10 years ago might not be your why today. Clearly define your why and you will have a better chance of obtaining it.

I wanted a million dollars by the time I reached 35. That could sum up what I wanted when I turned 30. No clear goal, all I knew was I wanted to be rich. Fast forward to about 10 years later. What do I want?

I want my bank account filled with enough money so I can have all my bills on autopay and never have to worry if I have enough money in my account to pay them.

A house with a couple of dogs, farm animals, a fresh garden, and an office for me and my wife. A pool, basketball court, baseball field, quads, dirt bikes, and fresh air.

But like anything in life, the good things take time. Time to develop, time to grow, and time to evolve. Most of us weren't born with a silver spoon in hand. We must work, learn and work some more.

If you don't have it yet, maybe it is because you wouldn't know what to do with it yet. You don't have the maturity you think you have, and you need to grow a little more.

I thought when I started this business, I was ready and prepared for anything. And really, I was immature. I was unseasoned. I didn't have the confidence to come through. Now I bleed confidence. And for good reason. I have learned a ton.

It's not how hard you work; it's how you strategize to build a company that makes you rich. I am sure you heard that hard work won't be done alone. Why do you think that is?

Let's look at a roofer in July. Or a roofer in December. It sounds like hard work in the elements because it is. If hard work got you Lamborghini, then we would have a lot more of them driving around town.

Strategy, products, employees. That is what will make you rich. Not hard work.

What is your why?

147

Chapter 23: Thank you

Thank you for taking the time to read this book. I know there are a lot of books out there. I hope this book was able to deliver at least one thing that will help you on your journey.

If you enjoyed the book, please consider leaving a good review. Reviews will help others know if this book is worth buying.

Like I said before, this book took me over a year to write. I am interested if anyone will like it.

Thanks for reading. I wish you the best of luck on your entrepreneurial journey. I look forward to hearing from you.

If you need anything from me, send me a message. I would be happy to help in any way I can.

PS, I got the cover done before I finished the book. I told the designer to make it for 150 pages. I guess when you get a book cover designed for the spine to look right you need a certain number of pages.

Use the last few blank pages to write down your thoughts.

149

150

www.ingramcontent.com/pod-product-compliance
Lightning Source LLC
Chambersburg PA
CBHW070021300526
45794CB00001B/383